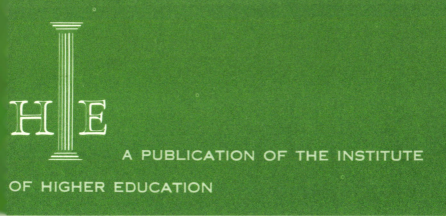

A PUBLICATION OF THE INSTITUTE
OF HIGHER EDUCATION

# LIBERAL EDUCATION

# AND SOCIAL WORK

GORDON J. ALDRIDGE

EARL J. McGRATH

TEACHERS COLLEGE, COLUMBIA UNIVERSITY

2)5 ⅄

# PUBLICATIONS OF
# THE INSTITUTE OF HIGHER EDUCATION

LIBERAL EDUCATION AND MUSIC
*Willis J. Wager* and *Earl J. McGrath*

LIBERAL EDUCATION AND BUSINESS
*William M. Kephart, James E. McNulty,* and *Earl J. McGrath*

LIBERAL EDUCATION AND HOME ECONOMICS
*Jeanette A. Lee* and *Paul L. Dressel*

THE ACADEMIC DEANSHIP
*John Wesley Gould*

COOPERATIVE LONG-RANGE PLANNING IN LIBERAL ARTS COLLEGES
*Earl J. McGrath*

THE PREDOMINANTLY NEGRO COLLEGES AND UNIVERSITIES IN TRANSITION
*Earl J. McGrath*

LIBERAL EDUCATION IN THE SERVICE ACADEMIES
*William E. Simons*

LIBERAL EDUCATION AND SOCIAL WORK
*Gordon J. Aldridge* and *Earl J. McGrath*

SELECTED ISSUES IN HIGHER EDUCATION
AN ANNOTATED BIBLIOGRAPHY
*L. Richard Meeth*

Copies of these reports may be purchased from the
Teachers College Press, Teachers College, Columbia University

# LIBERAL EDUCATION
# AND SOCIAL WORK

**GORDON J. ALDRIDGE**
*Director, School of Social Work*
*Michigan State University*

**EARL J. McGRATH**
*Executive Officer, Institute of Higher Education*
*Teachers College, Columbia University*

PUBLISHED FOR THE
*INSTITUTE OF HIGHER EDUCATION*

BY
*TEACHERS COLLEGE PRESS*
TEACHERS COLLEGE, COLUMBIA UNIVERSITY

361
Al24c

# FOREWORD

UNDER A GRANT FROM THE CARNEGIE CORPORATION OF NEW YORK THE Institute of Higher Education has in recent years conducted a series of studies of undergraduate professional schools. These inquiries have been concerned with the amount and kinds of instruction students in various professional curricula received in the liberal arts and sciences. One conclusion which can be drawn from the results of these analyses of the course structures in the various professional schools is that the proportion of technical and liberal arts courses varies widely from school to school and from field to field. That is, some graduates of curricula in Engineering, Business Administration, Journalism, Music, and Nursing have had a highly specialized undergraduate education with relatively little instruction in the liberal arts and science disciplines. Others, on the contrary, have been required or have elected to pursue broad programs in nonprofessional fields and have had less, but usually more basic, instruction in the technical subjects directly related to an occupation.

The schools of social work, the subject of this report, exhibit a sharp contrast to the other forms of professional education studied in this series. For, although some institutions offer undergraduate programs preparing for immediate employment, the majority require applicants for admission to have completed the requirements for a bachelor's degree. Moreover, practitioners in social work have for years strongly advocated a broad liberal education as preparation for graduate study and for practice. The professional schools of social work appeared, therefore, to present an opportunity to study the relationships between undergraduate education and the instruction provided in graduate professional schools. The field provided the opportunity to investigate specific relationships between the amount of instruction undergraduates received in the social sciences, the natural sciences, and the humanities, and the records they made in a graduate program in social work.

In initiating this project the advice of the officers of the Council on Social Work Education was sought and freely given. Through the several years while the project was in progress the Council was helpful in supplying information about various aspects of preparation for professional education in social work and in arranging for contacts with persons concerned with a broad range of related activities. The Council also assisted the Institute in securing Dr. Gordon J. Aldridge, Director of the School of Social Work at Michigan State University, to undertake major responsibility for the research and institutional visitations in connection with the study. His efforts were supplemented in various respects by the staff of the Institute of Higher Education, particularly Mr. Herman Kauz who made the laborious analyses of the transcripts from which the relationships between undergraduate and graduate study in social work were established.

The Institute owes a debt of gratitude to the Council on Social Work Education and to Dr. Aldridge for their assistance in this enterprise and also to the officers of the Carnegie Corporation of New York for the grant which made the study possible. The opinions expressed in this report, however, represent only the views of the authors. The report contains a considerable body of fact which should be helpful to the profession in evaluating policies and practices in social work education. The findings also raise a number of questions which this inquiry could not undertake to answer, indeed questions which were not intended to be answered. Nevertheless, serious matters of educational and of public policy require further objective study before existing practices can be assumed to rest on a scientifically determined basis.

Three matters deserve the most exacting study beyond the limits reached in this inquiry. First, the findings here reveal that the composition of the undergraduate's curriculum and the field of his major seem to have little bearing on his success in a graduate program in social work. Further, research is required to determine why students with a heavy concentration in the social sciences make no better records in graduate school courses in social work than those who major in other fields. Moreover, this study was handicapped by the fact that there were too few students who had had an undergraduate major in social work to permit valid generalizations, but the few cases which were studied show a high positive relationship between concentration in social work courses in the undergraduate years and success in graduate school. A matter of such obvious importance ought to be studied more extensively before the conclusion is reached that the student should major in a liberal arts subject rather than in social work.

In fact what is needed is objectively controlled experimentation in which various amounts of undergraduate instruction in social work are taken by students who then enter a graduate school where their accomplishments can be compared with those of other students with completely different preparation. In fact, if the results in other fields, medicine, for example, have any related significance some students should be admitted to a professional school of social work with two and three years of college preparation and their records in the professional programs then carefully analyzed and appraised.

Second, in view of the prolonged serious shortage of professionally trained social workers and the probable continuing demands in the field, experiments should be conducted with a variety of curricular arrangements and structures in order to determine whether some types of social work responsibilities could not be discharged by persons who have spent less than six years in formal preparation for their jobs. One limitation in this study, and in most others concerned with preparation for a career as a social worker, or for that matter as a physician, lawyer, or nurse, is the failure to relate all types of previous education and academic accomplishments to success as a practitioner. These studies usually correlate undergraduate factors such as the amount of study in the various disciplines or the grades received with grades received in professional school courses.

But a positive correlation between such factors does not prove a similar relationship between them and the efficient practice of a profession or enlightened citizenship. Specifically, a further investigation should be conducted into the relationship between the amount of preprofessional education, that is two, three, or four years, and the kinds of courses taken, on the one hand, and success in the actual practice of the social work occupations. Members of social work faculties are properly concerned with the problem of determining the types of undergraduate education which will assure the recipient that he will be able to pursue a graduate program in social work with success. They should be no less interested in discovering whether students who major intensively in English, sociology, physics, or social work as undergraduates, and achieve creditable standing, also later become highly competent practitioners in their vocation. Such questions cannot now be answered with any confidence. Consequently, additional research is very much needed if students are not to be unnecessarily burdened with additional years of education and the public not be denied of much-needed service.

Those concerned with social work education have been concerned about such matters through the years. The deans, the faculties, and the practitioners have demonstrated their interest in an objective assessment of social work education by their unreserved assistance in the various aspects of this study. They could make an additional contribution to the advancement of their profession by instigating broader and more intensive studies of the kind suggested by the findings of this report.

EARL J. MCGRATH
*Executive Officer*

# CONTENTS

# LIBERAL EDUCATION

# AND SOCIAL WORK

*Chapter 1*


# PROFESSIONAL EDUCATION FOR THE
# SECOND HALF OF THE TWENTIETH CENTURY*


THE EVENTS OF THE PAST SEVERAL YEARS HAVE SHARPLY FOCUSED AT-
tention on the purposes and the functions of American higher education.
Stimulated by the advances in science and technology in other parts of
the world, educators and laymen have become particularly concerned
with the merits of professional and technological education on the one
hand and liberal studies on the other, and even more with the relationships which should obtain between them.

The questions involved are ancient. In the fourth century B.C., Aristotle, commenting on the educational principles and practices of his
time, said: ". . . the existing practice [of education] is perplexing; no
one knows on what principle it should proceed—should the useful in
life, or should virtue, or should higher knowledge, be the aim of our
training; all three opinions have been entertained. Again, about the
means there is no agreement."[1] Ever since these ancient days partisans
of two main types of education—often called "professional" and "liberal"
—have defended their respective merits. The debate continues today
with renewed vigor, and for a number of reasons it is timely.

First, the general public is agitated by Russian advances in the fields
of science and technology. Many Americans are raising questions about
the reasons for what they rightly or wrongly consider to be the superiority
of the Russians in the type of education basic to their startling achieve-

---

*By Earl J. McGrath. The ideas in this chapter are considerably elaborated
and expanded in *Liberal Education in the Professions,* by Earl J. McGrath (New
York: Teachers College Press, Teachers College, Columbia University, 1959).

[1] Aristotle, *Politics* (New York: The Modern Library, 1943), p. 321.

1

ments in the sciences. Although the issues involved in these questions extend far beyond the boundaries of higher education, some of the more urgent problems as seen by many educators and thoughtful lawmen are related to the functions and programs of colleges and universities.

Those who advocate an intensification of education in the professional and semiprofessional vocations and in the fields of scholarship concerned with science have the onerous responsibility of describing how preparation for the other broad activities of life is to be adequately provided. Those, on the contrary, who stress the social and personal values of liberal education must realistically face the increasing need in the modern world for persons with advanced training in an occupational field—and show how this is to be furnished in increasing measure. The significance of occupational education can be appreciated only when it is realized that there are now twenty-two hundred occupations requiring highly trained manpower, and that ten to twenty more are created annually. As valuable as liberal arts education may be, it is not all that is needed by those employed in the specialized vocations. It is necessary and reasonable, therefore, to reconsider the full complement of educational services these workers must have if they are to be vocationally efficient and civically competent.

Second, for several decades the proportion of all college students attending professional units in colleges and universities has steadily mounted. Many of the present schools, such as those in business administration and social work, were inconspicuous, if not completely missing, in the total enterprise of higher education at the turn of the century. There were, for example, only three schools of business before 1900 and these enrolled a mere handful of students. Now tens of thousands of students attend several hundred such institutions. In 1900 there were no schools or departments of social work. Now 6,000 students attend 57 graduate schools of social work in the United States, several thousand are enrolled in 140 undergraduate departments offering a recognized core of social welfare courses,[2] and thousands of other undergraduate students take at least one social welfare course during their bachelor's program.

The growth of the college and university divisions devoted to the various forms of education directly related to an occupation is evident from the enrollments in these institutions. Dael Wolfle has shown that in 1901, of all the first degrees granted, the aggregate of those in business, agriculture, education, and engineering was only 4.1 per cent of the total awarded by all types of institutions.[3] By 1951–52, however, the figure

[2] Recognized by the Council on Social Work Education.
[3] Dael Wolfle, *America's Resources of Specialized Talent* (New York: Harper & Row, Publishers, 1954), p. 292.

had risen to 46.4 per cent, or almost half the first degrees awarded. If these students are to receive any education other than that which prepares them for their occupational activities, this general education must in some manner or other be made an integral part of the professional program. There are many issues in this merging of two sets of educational objectives which deserve thoughtful analysis on the basis of which systematic planning can take place.

Third, although the series of questions involved in establishing the proper proportions and relationships between the professional and the liberal education of college-going youth most obviously apply to the universities, those queries must also be answered by the faculties of liberal arts colleges. These older units in our system of higher education, like their sister institutions, have in the past several decades inaugurated a wide variety of professional and semiprofessional curricula. Another study conducted by the Institute of Higher Education[4] has revealed that some independent liberal arts colleges offer more than twenty vocationally oriented programs leading to one or another bachelor's degree, and that virtually all such institutions provide some instruction of this type. Moreover, the specialization in the various conventional liberal arts departments has now become so intense that to all intents and purposes these programs are no less vocational than their counterparts in schools of engineering, business administration, and education. If, therefore, the graduates of the liberal arts colleges are to leave these institutions adequately prepared to live intelligently and effectively in the larger sphere of life outside their occupations, the same questions which are matters of consideration in the separate professional schools must be raised concerning the relationship between general and specialized education in the liberal arts colleges.

Fourth, there is increasing concern among our citizens about the rising cost of higher education in money and in time. Medical education is the prime example of the steady lengthening of the course of formal study and the consequent increase of the financial burden on the student and his family. As late as 1900 young men could enter a medical school with no more than a secondary schooling and complete the medical course in two academic years considerably shorter than they are at present. Now the average for premedical and medical education is eight years, to which are added varying but usually long periods of internship or residency.

In some schools of education, nursing, pharmacy, and commerce, and in other professional fields as well, formal education has been ex-

---

[4] Earl J. McGrath and Charles H. Russell, *Are Liberal Arts Colleges Becoming Professional Schools?* (New York: Teachers College Press, Teachers College, Columbia University, 1958).

tended to five or six years. Professional social work preparation requires six years: four undergraduate and two graduate. Serious social problems are involved in the steady extension of pre-employment education. There are curtailments of earning capacity, maladjustments in personal and family life, and an often unrecognized selection of individuals whose parents are in the social and economic groups which can afford the large capital investment required to complete a long professional course of study. This investigation is only tangentially concerned with these latter matters. It is, however, directly concerned with the related question as to whether a more carefully considered plan for the total education of the individual, involving a clarification of the purposes and character of both liberal and professional education, could not keep the scope of higher education within more reasonable and defensible bounds.

Finally, the opportunities for adult education now provided by almost all institutions of higher education, and the opportunities for continuing education of high quality within commerce and industry, make necessary a re-examination of the amount and kind of higher education a prospective practitioner needs before he enters upon his intended life work. Considering the wealth of postgraduate educational opportunities now available, all baccalaureate curricula, both in professional schools and in liberal arts colleges, require critical reappraisal aimed at determining as objectively as possible which educational functions can most properly be performed before graduation and which can most profitably be conducted after the individual actually assumes his vocational responsibilities.

There, then, are the chief reasons for the studies of the curricula of professional units in colleges and universities. Before undertaking the detailed analyses of various institutional policies and practices which constitute the major purpose of this study, it was necessary to explore the meaning and purpose of liberal and professional studies and to establish a working basis for properly interrelating these two educational functions in an integrated whole.

Before considering the matters of fact and theory which are germane to a discussion of the structure and content of professional education, it should be observed that much of the early education in this country in all professional callings was narrowly technical. Most curricula in that day, and indeed up to very recent times, emphasized handbook information and rule-of-thumb procedures while neglecting basic theory and generalized knowledge useful in the infinitely varied circumstances of everyday practice. This kind of training was in fact *illiberal* in terms of any modern definition of either liberal or professional education. But this exclusive purpose of earlier professional programs—to make the individual technically competent—has now been largely replaced in theory if not in practice by the conception that all specialties must rest on a solid basis of theoretical knowledge and be practiced with the imaginative employment of general intellectual skills.

The most advanced views today assume that, if it is to be fully effective in preparing graduates for the complicated demands of contemporary life, professional education must have not a single goal but rather three comprehensive objectives. First, because of its very nature, it must obviously inculcate the corpus of knowledge, the complement of skills, and the traits of personality and character which constitute the distinctive features of a particular craft. It is these characteristics which give the profession its cohesiveness and identity. The celebrated psychologist William James, who, in his monumental *Principles of Psychology,* analyzed the attributes which differentiate one occupation from others, observed that "Already at the age of twenty-five you see the professional mannerism settling down on the young commercial traveler, on the young doctor, on the young minister, on the young counsellor-at-law." At one time, cultivating these distinguishing qualities of an occupational group was the sole purpose of its entire preparatory educational program. Today, however, at least the more forward-looking institutions consider two other aims as hardly less significant than that of equipping the student to perform effectively the duties of his chosen work.

A second purpose, and one of rising importance, is concerned with the general education which all those who attend an institution of higher education must have if they are to understand, and to live competently in, an increasingly complex democratic society. President John Hannah of Michigan State University expressed this newer conception when he told representatives of the land-grant colleges that "It is not enough that our young people be outstanding technicians. The first and never-forgotten objective must be that every product of our educational system must be given that training that will enable him to be an effective citizen, appreciating his opportunities and fully willing to assume his responsibilities in a great democracy."[5] Intelligent living today requires a knowledge of matters of domestic and international affairs infinitely more complicated and shifting than those of even a generation ago. Moreover, recent advances in the physical and biological sciences impinge so directly on the life of the average citizen that he cannot live capably today in ignorance of these arresting penetrations of the unknown regions of the physical world. The rapid growth of reliable knowledge in the physical and the social sciences

[5]John A. Hannah. "The Place of the Land-Grant College in the Public Educational System of the Future," *Proceedings of the Fifty-Eighth Annual Convention of the Association of Land-Grant Colleges and Universities,* Vol. 58 (1944), p. 76.

requires that the purposes of higher education for a vocation be extended beyond the bounds of technical knowledge or expertness in his own field.

Furthermore, an educational institution can hardly absolve itself of a third responsibility—that of assisting the student in gaining self-understanding, a moral grounding, and a consistent view of the world. In the words of the Committee on Aims and Scope of Engineering Education, the humanities and the social sciences have a responsibility to assist the student in the "development of moral, ethical, and social welfare and to a sound professional attitude."[6] Though a graduate may be ever so competent a practitioner and citizen, without knowledge of his own nature and a reasoned philosophy of life, he will fail to realize his full potential. Throughout his adult life the kaleidoscopic world around him will remain a meaningless flux of unrelated events. Recognizing the need for this philosophical orientation, many leaders in professional education appraise it as highly as professional skill and civic competence. In fact, one leader lists these three dominant purposes of journalism education in the following order: "(1) It should fit the student for being an effective citizen. (2) It should fit him for living a useful, full, satisfying life. (3) It should provide basic preparation for work in journalism."[7]

If these three comprehensive objectives of professional education are to be achieved, a judicious readjustment must be made in the balance of instruction directly related to the student's prospective occupation and instruction in the disciplines traditionally termed "the liberal arts and sciences." Before considering what types of readjustments are necessary, however, consideration must be given to the purposes of liberal arts education in order to determine to what extent and by what means they can be served in the curricula of professional schools.

What are the major purposes of liberal education in contemporary American society? Though it would doubtless be difficult, if not impossible to arrive at a generally acceptable definition of liberal education, perhaps a measure of agreement can be reached through a description of the types of abilities and personality traits which liberal education might be expected to engender in those who have been subject to its influences.

*First,* it would probably be generally agreed that those who have had a liberal education should have acquired a broad knowledge of the various major areas of learning—the natural sciences, the social sciences, and the humanities, including the fine arts. Though it is doubtless true, as White-

[6] Society for the Promotion of Engineering Education, Committee on Aims and Scope of Engineering Education, "Report," *Journal of Engineering Education,* Vol. 30 (March 1940), p. 564.

[7] Leslie G. Moeller, "Goals of Professional Education for Journalism," *The Quill,* Vol. 40 (August 1952), pp. 6 ff.

head observed, that "A merely well-informed man is the most useless bore on God's earth," it is no less true that today the ignorant are a menace to themselves and to their fellow citizens. No person can now live fully and effectively, according to Ortega y Gasset, without at least a modest knowledge of "the culture, the vital system of ideas, which the age has attained"—and Ortega meant the age in which the individual is living.

Yet it must be apparent to anyone who moves among "educated" people that some who leave our institutions of higher education today are unacquainted with the living ideas of their time. Haltingly they feel their way in darkness through many of the common avenues of life because their path is unilluminated by even the most elementary knowledge of many aspects of their own being or of the physical and social universe which surrounds them. That many who have spent four or more years in an institution of higher education are innocent of much of the reliable knowledge of their time is attested by the experiences of the author of a bestseller on the social implications of atomic energy. In discussions with college audiences he observed that on many matters of fundamental significance they were no better informed and hardly more curious than the man in the street.

In view of the enormous mass and accelerating rate of growth of knowledge, students cannot fairly be expected to encompass any large portions of it in four, or even in forty, years. They can, however, properly be expected to gain an acquaintance with the basic facts and principles of the various disciplines. A student who completes a professional education of four years or more with however distinguished a record in engineering, pharmacy, education, or agriculture, but with little or no knowledge of English literature, history, philosophy, or economics, is not liberally educated. He will be prepared to think and act effectively neither in his chosen occupation nor in the many life situations which are the common lot of all.

The mere possession of facts, however, does not guarantee the efficient, the incisive, and the imaginative use of the mind. Cardinal Newman, in his brilliant analysis of the nature of liberal education, *The Idea of a University,* has said:

> Knowledge then is the indispensable condition of expansion of mind and the instrument of attaining to it; this cannot be denied, it is ever to be insisted on; I begin with it as a first principle; however, the very truth of it carries men too far . . . the end of a Liberal Education is not mere knowledge.[8]

[8] John Henry Newman, *The Idea of a University* (New York: Longmans, Green and Co., 1955), p. 115.

*Second,* then, liberal education ought to cultivate those skills and habits of reasoning which constitute intellectual competence, the capacity to think logically and clearly, the ability to organize one's thoughts on the varied subjects with which the citizen today must unavoidably concern himself. In a sentence, these faculties might collectively be described as the capacity to order and interpret a complex set of circumstances in the physical, social, or artistic world, and to bring one's full intellectual resources skillfully to bear on the solution of a problem.

Just as the student must have some knowledge of many fields, so also, in order to gain competence in using the diverse forms of reasoning, he must have experience with intellectual processes other than those conventionally employed in his major academic field of interest. The various disciplines do, of course, employ some intellectual processes in common —the logical deduction of conclusions from valid premises, for example—whether the matter under consideration involves the facts of science, history, or art. Yet they also use intellectual methodologies in part peculiar to themselves. The chemist or physicist will only be satisfied with knowledge in which the probability of error is reduced to negligible proportions, while the historian or the sociologist, dealing as he does with human acts and events, must be satisfied with a much greater range of error of both fact and judgment. The student of art enjoys much greater freedom of subjective evaluation and interpretation than either the physical or the social scientist, but the intellectual processes by which he deals with reality are no less important than those employed by other disciplines.

The most distinctive and yet the most widely used processes of reasoning are doubtless the deductive method of formal logic and the inductive method of science. Those who are to be liberally educated can gain familiarity with these mental processes and skill in their use most readily by the study of mathematics and the sciences. No person can live intelligently today unless he understands the methods of reasoning with which scientists have so dramatically explored the unknown regions of the universe, from the boundless oceans of cosmic space to the infinitesimal region of the atom's nucleus. The intellectual procedures used in the conception of a hypothesis, the arrangement of an experiment to test it, the drawing of conclusions from the facts thus established—all these skills every citizen needs to acquire if he is to reason validly and objectively about physical phenomena. Moreover, properly taught, these habits of thought can be broadly applied in analyses of the complex social world with which all human beings are surrounded. Since the sciences differ in their use of these procedures with a wide variety of physical problems, the broadest range of acquaintance with these subjects will accomplish the fullest understanding and skill in the use of their methods.

Other branches of learning, the humanistic disciplines for example, use somewhat different intellectual operations in their interpretation of the world and the activities of men. Though they naturally employ the laws of logic in constructing a reasoned view of reality, their distinctive characteristic is their concern with values, with the ends of life, with the destiny of man. Those who teach history, literature, foreign languages, philosophy, and the arts cannot confine themselves to a consideration of the characteristics and behavior of exactly measurable phenomena. They must introduce the student to the reflections of creative minds on the nature of man and his world and their conclusions which are usually couched in much less precise terms than those of the scientist. The concern of teachers of these subjects must be with man, not as a physico-chemical complex within a mechanistically determined system, but rather as a being of purposes, values, loves, hates, and ideals—and sometimes as a seer or prophet with divine inspiration. In literature, the student should vicariously enjoy many of the richest experiences of life, gaining insight into human motivation and behavior attainable in no other way except through personal experience.

Still another area of human intellectual endeavor uses somewhat different approaches in its interpretation of reality. The social sciences— economics, sociology, and political science, for example—insofar as possible follow scientific procedure by constructing hypotheses, setting up experimental controls, and making accurate observations. These disciplines also use other investigative procedures, including statistical method, historical analysis, and case studies. Unlike the natural scientist, however, the scholar concerned with social phenomena often cannot arrange experiments which others can repeat. On the contrary, he must sometimes accept data of unprovable authenticity or of incomplete representativeness and, reasoning cautiously, arrive at tentative conclusions. Much of his material does not lend itself to the exact measurement used by the physical scientist. In the words of Taussig, one of this country's most celebrated economists, the social scientist is concerned with the "wavering and incalculable behavior" of man. The educated person must be skilled in these processes of tentative and precise reasoning about phenomena of inexact measurement. Most human actions must be based on evidence which, though not fully conclusive, is the best available at the time. One of the chief aims of higher education should be to cultivate habits which will prevent human beings from acting blindly, with no facts, and also from procrastinating indefinitely because the last shred of evidence is not in.

The liberally educated mind possesses another set of intellectual abilities, those involving the effective use of the various symbols and media of expression and communication. In the formulation of concepts and in the orderly development of a reasoned view of life, the meanings of words are the building blocks; the logical relationships among these verbal expressions, the cement which holds them together. No aspect of higher education has been more severely criticized than the teaching of the skills of communication. Yet instruction in this subject is highly valued by those who realize its importance in all phases of adult life. Several years ago this statement was well documented in a study of over thirteen thousand degree-holding employees of the General Electric Company. These graduates were divided into two groups, those who had attended engineering schools and those who were graduates of nonengineering curricula, mainly liberal arts colleges. When asked to appraise the various subjects they had pursued in undergraduate days in terms of their career value, the nonengineers placed English communication, both oral and written, at the top of the list, and this subject was placed second only to mathematics by the engineering graduates.[9]  The symbols of mathematics and of the arts, though not as widely and as frequently used by the ordinary citizen as words, are nevertheless essential elements in the lives of cultured men and women.

Equipped with essential knowledge and the skills of intellectual workmanship, the college graduate may nevertheless have failed to reach another important goal, perhaps the *sine qua non* of liberal education. Though richly informed, and capable of clear and cogent reasoning, he may yet be intolerant, unwise, intellectually stagnant, and inept in the arts of human association. The *third* major objective of liberal education is, therefore, concerned with attitudes, ideals, and traits of personality and character. These qualities, harder to describe and to measure than the other outcomes of liberal education, are yet the hallmark of the liberally educated person. As has been said, they are the qualities that remain with the individual after all the facts which were learned have been forgotten.

The liberally educated person embraces certain values. He has at least a provisionally formed and examined philosophy of life, a *Weltanschauung*, a religion around which he organizes the varied purposes and activities of his existence. These values of the liberally educated man represent not only the ideas and causes for which he would live, but more importantly those for which if necessary he would die. They give stability to his being. They serve to keep the ship of life steady on course as it is buffeted by the unpredictable forces of man and of nature. Without

[9] "What They Think of Their Higher Education, A Report of a Survey of the Opinions of 13,586 College Graduates, Employees of the General Electric Company," *Educational Relations Bulletin* (January 1957).

them the lives of men have no direction, for, as Socrates said, "If a man does not know to what port he is sailing, no wind is favorable."

Knowing his limitations, the liberally educated man has respect for the rights and views of others. He is humble, not only before the capricious and uncontrollable forces of man and of nature, but also in the presence of his own ignorance. And most important of all, he continually seeks wisdom through the extension of his knowledge and reflection on its meanings. Realizing how much he does not know, he is driven by an unrelenting curiosity, an unquenchable thirst for deeper knowledge and fuller understanding. Unless professional education inspires the desire to learn, to extend the scope of one's knowledge, to increase one's insights into the nature of things, it has condemned its recipients to eventual ignorance and mental stagnation. For the explosive increase of knowledge is the most arresting fact in today's world of learning, and swiftly accelerating change the most characteristic feature of modern life.

Even if higher education were able to supply each student with all the knowledge needed to understand the world in which he currently lives, and even if it could sharpen the intellectual skills to a fine point, it would have failed if it had not added to these achievements the inculcation of the irresistible desire to learn and to know. For as knowledge grows and the world changes, all who wish to live intelligently must continue to grow and to change through learning. Unless education initiates a chain reaction in which each advance in understanding sets off the desire for greater growth in wisdom, those who leave our campuses will soon reach a state of permanent intellectual rest. They will lose touch with the ongoing world.

The purposes and character of professional education require a similarly intensive and critical analysis. Since, however, the remainder of this volume is concerned with a review of attitudes of faculty members and administrative officers, and of the practices in selected institutions with respect to this matter, only general guide lines for the development of a professional curriculum will be suggested at this point.

The dominant principle to be applied in determining the character and content of a professional program has to do with the degree of specialization the curriculum may be expected to provide. The substance of a professional course of study, and the manner in which it is organized and presented, must be decided in terms of the vast bulk of modern knowledge, its rate of growth and change, the time available to the average student for pre-employment training, and especially the proper purposes of initial education in a vocation. As these various factors which irresistibly shape professional education are analyzed, the dominant principle in curriculum construction is thrown into high relief. It becomes axiomatic that the student can be, and in principle should be, given only enough basic specialized instruction related to a vocational field to qualify him for initial gainful employment. W. Earl Armstrong sets forth this controlling idea in relation to teacher education, for example, when he says:

> It is not assumed that the pre-service curriculum should attempt to provide all of the insights and skills that the teacher will need in order to be a fully competent person. Rather, the function of the pre-service curriculum as here assumed is to provide the best possible preparation for the teacher to *begin* to teach. A pre-service curriculum based on this assumption will of necessity leave all aspects of the teacher's education incomplete. That is to say, the general education of the teacher will need further strengthening, the area or areas of subject-matter concentration will need either further broadening or deepening, and further additions will need to be made to the professional insights and skills of the teacher.[10]

If the several values in a professional curriculum are to be kept in proper balance, the student cannot be prepared as an expert in any specific job. Formal instruction can be expected to do no more than acquaint him with the vocabulary and the basic principles of a broad field such as pharmacy, engineering, or nursing, and cultivate the intellectual skills by means of which new knowledge can be acquired and applied to the infinitely varying problems of day-to-day practice. This conception of the scope of a professional school's purposes has been well expressed by Dean Helen Nahm of the School of Nursing at the University of California:

> I think our major problem in a professional school . . . is that we must, in a period of time which seems reasonable to students and their parents, prepare both a liberally educated person and a person with competencies essential for beginning practice in a professional field.

Cogent reasons support the view that a professional curriculum should embrace only those learning experiences necessary to orient the student broadly in his chosen occupation without aiming to cultivate a high degree of competence in any of its specialized branches.

The store of detailed knowledge in any professional field is enormous, and it expands prodigiously. This accelerating growth of fact and theory, the invariable characteristic of every intellectual realm, explains why no one can become or remain a genuine expert in a specialized branch of learning except by long years of study and by continually renewed acquaintance with evolving fact, principle, technique, and practice. It is

[10] W. Earl Armstrong. "The Teacher Education Curriculum," *The Journal of Teacher Education,* Vol. 8, No. 3 (September 1957), p. 232.

for this reason that even those who, for example, graduate from a school of business administration with distinction and with the beginning of a specialization in management or retailing are nevertheless given positions relatively low in the structure of business enterprise.

Second, highly specialized instruction fails to reach its reputed goal because each set of circumstances in professional life has its own peculiar structure. To a degree it involves concepts and techniques which vary from those of all other situations. Consequently, the principles of accounting, orchestration, *materia medica,* educational psychology, or social work must be adapted to the special circumstances and needs of a particular situation. The beginner who takes up his duties in any profession prepared to apply a specific body of detailed facts or procedures to new sets of circumstances will find his bag of tricks hopelessly inadequate. Unfortunately, he will only then belatedly realize that in concentrating excessively on a narrow specialty he has failed to gain the flexibility of mind and personality required to understand and to deal effectively with a host of important matters both professional and otherwise. Inevitably he will lack breadth in both general and professional knowledge and in the intellectual skills essential to their profitable use in the varied patterns of professional exigencies.

In the making of a professional curriculum, another guiding principle is related to the technical courses themselves. Those who have considered the matter most studiously are convinced that *even professional instruction* should stress broad principles, key ideas, and overarching generalizations rather than detailed facts and techniques. Here it is profitable to raise questions concerning what kind of education is of most worth, and how much can be accomplished in the time available.

The curricula of forward-looking engineering schools, for example, provide convincing illustrations of successful efforts to place greater emphasis on principles than on techniques, thus making possible the enlargement of the general education component and a broader orientation in the vocational field itself. Even in the engineering subjects many schools have adopted a core program of professional subject matter as the common basis of the specialties such as civil, chemical, electrical, and mechanical engineering. The enlargement of these common components has been possible only through the dropping of some specialized instruction which in earlier years pre-empted a considerable portion of the four-year curriculum. This shift in emphasis has increased the student's knowledge of theoretical engineering and of the liberal arts disciplines, thus enhancing both his occupational and his civic competence.

Another principle to be applied in designing a professional course of study relates to the cultivation of attitudes and motivations which are not the sole concern of any subject-matter field but rather the responsibility of all. Proposals for the reconstruction of professional curricula will succeed or fail largely to the extent that students are helped to recognize formal education as only the beginning rather than the end of a long process of personal growth. Unless the experiences of the college years are viewed in this light the student is likely to misconceive the aims of higher education. Not uncommonly, faculty members and curriculum makers encourage students' misconceptions of the purposes and the potential of undergraduate education. A subconscious feeling, subtly transferred to those under instruction, that they must "learn it now or never" is the origin of the common compulsion to include every last bit of information, to explore every remote corner of the subject, in a single course. Under the influence of this point of view all curricula have become swollen with masses of dispensable facts, and the atmosphere of the classroom has become one of hurried absorption of facts rather than of reflective analysis and the orderly expansion of mind.

A curriculum with the proper objectives ought to provide the basic experiences needed by the neophyte to begin his practice with a sufficient body of knowledge to give him confidence in his own ability and to make possible further professional growth through individual study, practice, and additional part-time instruction in so-called "refresher" courses. He ought to have the flexibility of mind to pursue and to accept additions to knowledge and innovations in procedures as they appear. He ought also to have a vision of the wider significance of his work in the whole social context of his time. More than this an undergraduate and perhaps a graduate program cannot and need not be expected to accomplish.

The achievement of these two sets of purposes for a responsible and full life as a private citizen and as a member of an occupational group is an ambitious undertaking. Yet, under proper conditions it is not an unrealistic goal. Our national and personal welfare demand that it be reached within the next decade; our needs for highly skilled workers and for informed and active citizens are patently urgent.

If these aims are to be realized, however, certain of the presently controlling ideas and practices in American higher education require reassessment. Many of the graduates of institutions of higher education will not reach these goals if it is assumed that only those disciplines commonly classified under the caption "liberal arts" have these desiderata as their aims. On the contrary, much of the instruction in professional curricula such as engineering, business administration, education, nursing, and social work must be expected (as it already lives up to the expectation) to cultivate the qualities of mind and character often considered the exclusive province of the liberal arts.

No one has better described the possibility of achieving the ends of liberal education through the study of specialized subjects than President Virgil M. Hancher of the State University of Iowa, who at a meeting of the Association of Land-Grant Colleges and Universities in 1953 said:

> We forget that it is possible to become liberally educated by the teaching and study of professional or specialized subjects in a liberal manner. . . .
>
> While in general I would support the proposition that there are some things which every liberally educated man should know, I fear that we have been led into error sometimes by believing that the study of certain subject matter inevitably results in a liberal education. This is a doubtful proposition. It is nearer to the truth to say that there is no subject matter, worthy of a place in the curriculum of a modern Land-Grant College or state university, which cannot be taught either as a professional specialty or as a liberal subject.[11]

It is obvious that courses in engineering or pharmacy, if properly taught, acquaint the student with a wide range of scientific facts and cultivate the intellectual skills of the scientist. They also instill a respect for truth, a humbleness of spirit, a desire to learn, and the habit of philosophical reflection about the place of man in a limitless cosmos. The same can be said for instruction in other professional programs, though the emphasis on particular subject matter and skills would obviously vary with the field concerned.

Engineering can be used to illustrate how a rounded education can be provided for the student in a professional course of study. The first objective of liberal education, acquainting the student with the fundamental facts and principles in the three main areas of knowledge, can be accomplished by supplementing the basic courses in science with instruction in the social sciences, the humanities, and the skills of communication. The requirements in the social sciences and the humanities ought to be met by the pursuit of courses especially designed to bring the student into touch with the leading principles and the key ideas in a broad range of subjects not included in courses in engineering and basic science.

In the social sciences, for example, such subjects might include history, political science, sociology, and economics. Courses should be unlike conventional elementary courses in that no attempt should be made

---

[11] Virgil M. Hancher, "Liberal Education in Professional Curricula," *Proceedings of the Sixty-Seventh Annual Convention of the American Association of Land-Grant Colleges and State Universities,* Columbus, Ohio, November 10–12, 1953 (Washington, D.C.: The Association, 1953), pp. 45–51.

to cover all the detailed knowledge necessary for advanced study. Instead, selected topics ought to be studied intensively, so that the study would emphasize relationships between the constituent disciplines, and inculcate skill in the use of the methods of thought employed in dealing with social problems. Thus the second objective of cultivating intellectual skills in the social sciences would be accomplished. Comparable instruction in literature, languages, philosophy, and the arts should acquaint the student with the content and methods of the humanities. Since scientific subjects are necessarily basic to specialized engineering courses, it could be assumed that all students would have gained a considerable knowledge of science and skill in the use of its methods.

The third objective of liberal education, that of cultivating the attitudes and the traits of character which signalize the liberally educated mind, must necessarily be the responsibility of all teachers of all subjects. Any subject can be taught so as to increase the student's respect for truth and for the worth of the individual, his appreciation of his own smallness in our vast universe, and his love of wisdom and desire to learn. For this reason, as Hancher holds, courses of study cannot on the basis of content or method alone be classified as liberal, and courses in colleges of liberal arts which do not have these aims can surely not be described as liberal.

The graduate of such a program in engineering would possess not only the knowledge of his world at large and the aptitude to use his intellectual resources in expanding his learning. He would be capable of seeing his own occupational activities in the larger social context of his time. Similar curricular arrangements are feasible in all other professional schools. The general principle of curriculum construction involved is that the two **major** areas of knowledge not basic to the professional subject matter be adequately represented by appropriate general instruction. In business administration, for example, these would be the humanities and the natural sciences; in agriculture, the social sciences and the humanities; in music, the natural and the social sciences; and so on for all the other professions. Whether these broad purposes of liberal education will really be achieved will depend on the teachers. A course in finance, for example, taught with emphasis on general economic principles, with consideration for the historical development and the present importance of financial institutions in Western society, and with constant reference to the interrelationship of money and banking with the facts of sociology, anthropology, political science, and psychology, not to mention ethics and art, will have many of the values of liberal education, whatever its uses may be in educating a student for employment in the world of commerce. Conversely, a course in Greek literature with an emphasis on dates, literary style, linguistic analysis, and the esoteric subject matter of the teacher's research on some peculiar characteristic of Greek grammar, may produce few of the desirable results of liberal study. The teacher and the preparation he receives for his responsibilities in the classroom are, always have been, and always will be the decisive factor in liberal or, for that matter, any other kind of education. The present inadequacies in American higher education, particularly in its failure to preserve the heritage of liberal culture, have their origin in the attitudes, purposes, and skills of the teachers. Many teachers—whether in professional schools or liberal arts colleges—in their preoccupation with the cultivation of specialized knowledge and the techniques of their own chosen narrow field of intellectual activity, have lost sight of the inclusive purposes of the upper level of undergraduate education.

Professional schools which adopt a broader set of objectives and make the requisite changes in their practices to bring them into conformity with these principles will provide more fully that generous education required by this generation to live more intelligently in the complex contemporary world. They will contribute more fully to the enrichment and the strengthening of this democratic society in which high production is of undeniable importance in peace and in war, but of no more pressing urgency or greater significance than informed citizenship and self-knowledge. As institutions generally adopt the pattern already in effect among the most enterprising, the ideal of education for high professional competence, for informed and active citizenship, and for a rich and integrated personal life will be within reach of all students in professional schools. It is to the realization of these ideals that these institutions might well dedicate themselves in this period when our people, with an eye to the ultimate destiny of our nation, are reassessing all of American education.

*Chapter 2*


# THE EVOLUTION OF EDUCATION FOR SOCIAL WORK

IN THE EARLIER INSTITUTE STUDIES OF PROFESSIONAL EDUCATION A BASIC study format was used for comparative purposes. Since social work is the only one of these fields in which professional education is wholly at the graduate level, this study was approached somewhat differently: Rather than (as with the other studies) considering the relationship of liberal and professional education within the undergraduate professional school, attention was centered on undergraduate liberal education *as preparation for* graduate social work education. Although this new dimension was introduced, it remained practicable to carry out the study within essentially the established format.

## PURPOSE, SCOPE, AND METHODOLOGY

Before stating its objectives, it is important to establish what the study is not. It is not a social work curriculum study such as those directed by Hollis[1] and Boehm.[2] It is not a study of social work education per se. It is not a study of social work practice.

It is a study of facts, attitudes, and expectations about undergraduate liberal education as preparation for graduate social work education in the United States. Although the inquiry is focused on undergraduate education, the findings may have implications for possible changes or shifts of emphasis in the graduate curriculum. The report reflects the thinking of representative social work educators and selected practitioners about cur-

[1] Ernest V. Hollis and Alice L. Taylor, *Social Work Education in the United States* (New York: Columbia University Press, 1951).
[2] Werner W. Boehm, *et al., The Social Work Curriculum Study,* 14 volumes (New York: Council on Social Work Educaton, 1959).

18

rent and future developments in the total program of social work education—undergraduate and graduate.

The study involved several kinds of inquiry, which were preceded by a series of letters from the Institute and the Council to the schools and departments of social work outlining the project and seeking their participation. Almost all the graduate schools and most of the undergraduate departments took part in at least one phase of the inquiry.

PHASES OF THE STUDY

*Bibliography.* An extensive but selected and annotated bibliography was prepared, covering the historical development and present status of liberal education in its relationships to professional social work study.[3] A memorandum was sent to each graduate social work school and undergraduate department with a social welfare concentration, and to chairmen of the 156 chapters in the National Association of Social Workers, seeking assistance in gleaning the literature in social work and related areas. Many persons submitted helpful lists of references, and some authors supplied annotations for their own publications.

*Attitude Inventory.* A second type of inquiry was concerned with a statistical analysis of the attitudes of three groups of persons in social work toward undergraduate liberal education as preparation for social work education:

1. *Graduate faculty:* all (744) full-time faculty members in the fifty-six graduate schools of social work in the United States
2. *Undergraduate faculty:* the 116 persons (one in each department) responsible for the social welfare concentration in the undergraduate departments recognized by the Council on Social Work Education[4]
3. *Practicing social workers:* the chairmen of the 156 chapters of the National Association of Social Workers

This analysis was made through a questionnaire—Inventory of Views in Regard to the Relationship of Liberal Education to Specialized Education—which was developed by the Institute of Higher Education for its previous studies of professional fields, in each of which preparatory professional education is commonly concluded in the undergraduate years. It should be pointed out, however, that increasingly graduate schools of

---

[3] See Appendix for a listing of these bibliographical items.

[4] *Undergraduate Departments of Colleges and Universities: Offering Courses with Social Welfare Content* (New York: Council on Social Work Education, July 1962).

business administration, engineering, and other professional units offer programs which stretch from freshman year through the master's or doctor's degree. In this study portions of the original inquiry materials which were not applicable for graduate faculty members were appropriately modified or dropped. The parts that were applicable provided a useful indication of views on undergraduate liberal education as it is related to graduate social work education.

Most of the inventory could be answered by the faculty members of the undergraduate departments of social work. Fewer sections were applicable for the social work practitioners; for this group an additional brief questionnaire was provided, seeking identifying data as well as information about each respondent's social work experience. The statistical information and general comments produced by these inquiries were analyzed and also compared with those from the eight professional fields studied earlier by the Institute of Higher Education.

*Transcript Analysis.*    A third phase of the study concerned the analysis of undergraduate and graduate transcripts of the class which received the MSW degree in June 1961. Each school was requested to select at random every eighth such student and to forward a copy of his complete undergraduate and graduate transcripts.

One of the primary purposes of this part of the study was to determine any relationship of kind, quality, and proportion of undergraduate liberal arts education and general level of undergraduate performance, to achievement in a graduate school of social work. Toward this end, the undergraduate courses in each transcript were identified within the following categories: natural sciences, humanities, social sciences (with a subcategory for sociology), social welfare, applied fields (other than social work), miscellaneous. The transcripts were also grouped according to the length of time between the awarding of the bachelor's degree and the beginning of study for the master's degree in the following interval periods: (1) up to two years, (2) from two to ten years, and (3) over ten years.

*School Visits.*    The fourth phase consisted of visits to nine of the 56 accredited schools of social work, selected to give a reasonable range according to such criteria as geographical location, size, age, and auspices. The institutions visited were Bryn Mawr College, University of California (Berkeley), Fordham University, University of Hawaii, Indiana University, Rutgers University, Tulane University, Wayne State University, and West Virginia University. In addition, the catalogs of all 56 schools were examined.

Visiting these schools also offered an opportunity for contact with undergraduate social welfare programs, since five of the nine schools either have or are developing a recognized core of undergraduate social welfare courses, and three others offer at least one undergraduate social welfare course.

During these two- or three-day visits inquiries were made among university and school administrative officers, faculty members, and students concerning their attitudes toward instruction in the various liberal arts fields and its place in the total education of future social work practitioners. Attention was also given to the forces on campuses which seemed to strengthen or weaken both liberal arts and professional programs, and to predispose the local faculty toward interest in broad or narrow professional education.

To contribute toward consistency of approach to each of these schools, a schedule (modified for social work) used in the Institute's other studies served as a guide. All "opinion" items were discussed with each faculty member. Factual items were discussed with the person or persons responsible for those items. Seven of the schools were visited by the study's consultant, the eighth was visited by the study director, and the ninth by both the director and the consultant.

The foregoing types of information provided the basic data which are reported in the following pages.

### HISTORICAL SETTING

Although professional social work is generally considered a twentieth-century and primarily North American phenomenon, it loses perspective if seen outside the historical framework of social welfare on this continent and in Europe. Some form of meeting social and personal needs has probably been with us as long as men have lived together in groups. From more or less well-intentioned efforts to temper human distress, social work has emerged as a professional activity through which help may be given to those in need in a purposeful and enlightened way.

Until the seventeenth century the church remained the chief source of this helping function, supplemented by usually haphazard local public and private aid. The tendency was toward a somewhat repressive giving or withholding of help on the basis of "worthiness," and the help was largely confined to material goods.

The indiscriminate giving of alms seemed to increase rather than reduce the problems arising out of rapid industrial expansion. The Elizabethan Poor Laws had attempted to bring order out of the chaos of public relief, but it remained for the German community experiments of the eighteenth and nineteenth centuries to develop the beginnings of an organized system of private welfare. By 1869 this system had reached England and was incorporated in the Charity Organization Society. The Society, also established in the United States a few years later, was a crucial development in the history of social work. In addition to its functions of coordination and investigation, it stimulated the growing concern with the theory and practice of personal service and responsibility. The steady expansion of the Society and other welfare organizations in the United States demanded increasing numbers of workers able to offer constructive help. It was becoming clear that it was not sufficient to be well intentioned and interested in people. Nor was it even sufficient to be able to give "enough" help. It was evident that the way in which the help was offered was important. The concept of relationship was not yet understood, but it was realized that the feeling between the worker and the person being helped was of significance. The need for some formalization of knowledge and training was being recognized.

STAGES IN PROFESSIONAL EDUCATION

Previous studies carried out by the Institute of Higher Education have identified five stages in the growth of professional education in the United States: the apprentice, proprietary school, university school, preprofessional requirement, and general education stages.[5]

The first of these, the apprentice stage, was marked within social work as in most professions by the learning on the part of the beginner through observation of and identification with an experienced worker. In the final quarter of the nineteenth century this became somewhat more formalized through training courses, institutes, and workshops occasionally carried on within the agency.

For the second stage, that of the proprietary school, there has been no real equivalent in the development of social work education. The agency-based course may be analogous, and is best illustrated by the summer training course given in 1898 by the Charity Organization Society of New York. Social work education is usually thought of as having its beginnings at this time.

The university school stage has normally been the third phase in the development of education for the professions in the United States. In social work there was an intermediate stage between the proprietary and university schools—that of the independent school. It had a formal program, but was not affiliated with a university. An illustration is the de-

    [5] Earl J. McGrath, *Liberal Education in the Professions* (New York: Teachers College Press, Teachers College, Columbia University, 1959), pp. 29–33.

velopment of the above summer training course into a one-year program in 1904 within the New York School of Philanthropy, which later became the New York School of Social Work and was ultimately affiliated with Columbia University.

Development of the university school is well illustrated by the Institute of Social Science which was established within the extension division of the University of Chicago. The independent School of Civics and Philanthropy which emerged from this institute ultimately became the first school to be fully integrated within a university and is now the School of Social Service Administration of the University of Chicago.

Most of the early schools were agency-sponsored with instruction largely given by agency executives. Much of the instruction remained apprenticeship training within an agency setting, supplemented by a limited amount of classroom instruction and reading. Only gradually did the agency experience develop some educational focus.

The fourth and fifth phases—the preprofessional requirement stage and the general education stage—are not clearly differentiated within the evolution of education for social work. However, the fourth stage is somewhat paralleled in social work by the requirement—more often now stated as a "preference" in the catalogs of schools of social work—that the aspiring professional student have had undergraduate courses in certain areas, particularly in the social sciences.

The general education stage, as recommended preparation for graduate social work education, is today the general rule. The majority of catalogs of schools of social work make explicit reference to the importance of a liberal undergraduate education. That this is not simply a gesture is attested by the overwhelming response in favor of liberal education as preparation for graduate social work education obtained through the Attitude Inventory responses. This was supported in depth by the interviews with faculty members in the nine graduate schools visited.

The professional education of social workers has evolved through these five stages during a sixty-five-year period. The development has not been even and always harmonious, but it has been related to developments within the profession and within higher education generally. The early years of the twentieth century were marked also by important discoveries in the fields of medicine, psychology, and sociology. Social work was beginning to move beyond the confines of the social agency and into working relationships with other professions, notably psychiatry.

The growth of knowledge and the increasing recognition that effective social work practice required deliberate preparation helped the existing schools to face the importance of establishing consistency and coordination of training efforts. In 1919 these seventeen schools organized the Association of Training Schools for Professional Social Work, renamed in 1924 the American Association of Schools of Social Work, serving the schools in both the United States and Canada. This organization remained the standard-setting and accrediting body for social work education until 1952. At this time it joined with other social work educational and professional organizations to form the Council on Social Work Education.

EARLY CURRICULUM DEVELOPMENTS

During the early years of the accrediting and coordinating association, the schools continued to operate programs widely disparate in content and presentation. Not until 1932 was a genuine effort made to standardize course offerings by the twenty-four member schools. A "minimum curriculum" was agreed upon in which certain courses would be offered to all students.

By 1935 the organization had agreed that a school must be affiliated with an accredited college or university, and by 1939 that professional education be graduate education with the master's degree awarded on completion of two years of study.

The years since 1940 represent not only the bringing together of knowledge gained from the biological and social sciences, but also the bringing together of the common denominators of different areas of social work. Within both social work practice and social work education there has been a growth in objectivity, characterized by more selective use of psychoanalytic theory and of concepts from allied disciplines, particularly cultural anthropology.

This parallel growth in practice and education has been reflected in several ways during the past twenty years. A milestone was passed in 1944 when the American Association of Schools of Social Work adopted a new curriculum policy which prescribed a core of eight course areas: casework, group work, community organization, research, medical information, psychiatric information, public welfare, and administration. This was a large step forward from the 1932 "minimum curriculum" where the concern had been with individual courses rather than with content areas.

The 1944 curriculum policy resulted essentially in a basic first year, but the second year remained specialized, differing according to a school's special resources and interests. The evolution of social work may be unique in this respect among the professions, most of which moved from general to specific practice. Social work first developed specialized fields of practice—with specific requirements within social work education for these—and with their own accreditation standards and procedures. Social work only later moved toward generic practice and education. This movement was accelerated by the adoption of a social work curriculum policy statement in 1952, and by the merging of the seven professional associations into the National Association of Social Workers in 1955. Approval of specialized programs in social work education was discontinued in 1959.

A major development was the publication in 1951 of a report of a comprehensive study of social work education.[6] This study was carried out by the National Council on Social Work Education which had been created in 1946 as a coordinating and study group to try to resolve the difficulties raised by having two accrediting bodies concerned with social work education: the American Association of Schools of Social Work and the National Association of Schools of Social Administration.

This latter organization had been formed in 1942 by a number of universities and colleges offering a combined undergraduate-graduate type of social work training. Its membership requirements indicated a curriculum primarily at the undergraduate level in at least one of the following fields: social work, employment service, rural welfare, recreation, social insurance, guidance, rehabilitation, and personnel work. By 1950 the Association included thirty-two institutions and had developed accreditation standards. Since these standards were different from those established by the American Association of Schools of Social Work, it became increasingly difficult to develop a consistent and stable educational base for professional practice.

### THE HOLLIS-TAYLOR REPORT

The Hollis-Taylor report made a number of recommendations, the most important being accepted by the two associations, including the recommendation leading to their merger, along with the National Council on Social Work Education, into the newly-formed Council on Social Work Education.

This report was a thoughtful and provocative inquiry into the basic issues in social work education. Its careful reading is essential to an understanding of the development of social work education. The following summary prepared by Alice L. Taylor[7] outlines its major points:

[6] Ernest V. Hollis and Alice L. Taylor, *op. cit.*
[7] In Ernest F. Witte, "Social Work Education in the United States: A Review," *Child Welfare,* Vol. 31 (June 1952), p. 8.

The purpose of social work education is to prepare for professional responsibility that is broader than practice which is usually defined as direct services to individuals and groups.

Social work education is the responsibility of the whole profession—the educators, practitioners, membership organizations, social agencies and regulatory bodies.

The public has a stake in the kind of social work education that is provided as this determines largely the nature and caliber of services to the communities.

The growing edge of practice and the course of events in the field determine new developments in education.

Education for social work is a continuous process from the foundation laid in the undergraduate years, through graduate professional study, continuing in agency experience and staff training, and going on again in postgraduate study and in the stimulation in professional association and responsibility.

The school of social work should have the same status as other professional schools within the organization through financial support, and in the university councils that shape educational policy; it has much to gain, but also much to give.

Social work has made distinctive contributions to professional education and to the literature of casework and supervision. One contribution is how to develop and use the self in a disciplined professional way. This should be of significance to established and newer professions with a large component of human relations in their way of working.

Social work today rests largely on professional convictions and empirical experience and has yet to document these beliefs by research in practice and education.

Only as the scope and content of basic social work education are clearly identified will it be possible to determine questions about specialization in practice and education for the future.

Concepts, not courses, are the units for curriculum revision related to the needs of practice as the profession of social work further identifies its distinctive place in society.

An undergraduate concentration in social work should not include the teaching of professional skills.

### COUNCIL ON SOCIAL WORK EDUCATION

A direct outgrowth of this study was the formation of the Council on Social Work Education on July 1, 1952. The Council provides for representation from graduate schools of social work, undergraduate colleges and universities, employing agencies, the National Association of Social Workers, and the interested public. Its basic purpose is to promote the development of sound programs of social work education in the United States and Canada, and this purpose is implemented through its activities in accreditation, consultation, interpretation, recruitment, research, publications, and special services. At the final business meetings of the American Association of Schools of Social Work held in 1952 the member schools adopted a new statement of curriculum policy and the newly formed Council inherited the important function of promoting sound curriculum development in the graduate schools in the light of this new curriculum policy statement. The statement placed emphasis on the two-year social work curriculum as a cohesive whole and moved from a consideration of courses to a concern with three major subject areas.

The three areas were: Human Growth and Behavior, concerned with knowledge and understanding of the normal life cycle of man in society and with the deviations from this norm; the Social Services, concerned with knowledge and understanding of social welfare policy, structure, programs, and the organizations created to administer them; and Social Work Practice, concerned in both class and field with the professional methods used in carrying out social work functions. Noted within the third area but with implications for the total curriculum was the significance of the role of the field instructor as educator rather than supervisor.

The evolution from the first minimum curriculum to the 1952 policy statement has been described succinctly:

> The 1932 "minimum curriculum" represented a compromise among competing courses and conflicting educational objectives, that is, vocational training versus professional education; the 1944 "basic eight" represented agreement upon a core of courses; the 1952 statement represented agreement upon areas of knowledge and sequences that form a total two-year curriculum. Thus, each marks an important stage in the development of social work education.[8]

### NATIONAL ASSOCIATION OF SOCIAL WORKERS

During the 1950's, several important developments took place which had profound implications for social work education. Of particular significance was a major achievement in the development of the profession

---

[8] Katherine A. Kendall, "A Conceptual Framework for the Social Work Curriculum of Tomorrow," *Social Service Review,* vol. 27 (March 1953), p. 17.

of social work. In 1955 the seven existing professional associations—American Association of Group Workers, American Association of Medical Social Workers, American Association of Psychiatric Social Workers, American Association of Social Work, National Association of School Social Workers, Social Work Research Group, and the Association for the Study of Community Organization—merged into a single professional association: the National Association of Social Workers. This was the fulfillment of a seven-year process of conference and discussion between the professional organizations and reflected, among other things, a recognition that in the interests of optimum strength and clarity the time had come for social work to be professionally united.

The National Association of Social Workers, with a current membership of 42,000 professional persons, has continued a steady and progressive development. While its major concern is with social work practice, the Association plays an important educational role through its committees and chapters, as well as through its participation in the work of the Council on Social Work Education.

The merger of the seven former associations was logical from the viewpoint of the schools of social work. The accreditation of specialized programs within social work education had already passed to the former American Association of Schools of Social Work in the late 1940's. Continuing discussion by the schools of the maturation of social work education and practice from specialized to generic programs, led to the decision to discontinue the approval of specialized programs, effective July 1, 1959. Under the new policy, a school of social work would be accredited for its basic curriculum only.

### The Curriculum Study

Another major undertaking during these years was also concerned with curriculum. From the first comprehensive study of professional preparation for social work,[9] questions and issues in curriculum development had emerged requiring further exploration. The Council on Social Work Education accepted responsibility for undertaking such a study and, supported by grants from foundations, national agencies, and federal departments, initiated a three-year study of the social work curriculum in October 1955. The study staff, under the leadership of Dr. Werner W. Boehm, thought that some answers to the many questions might emerge through focusing on curriculum planning rather than by piecemeal consideration of the specific questions. Answers were sought to three

[9] Hollis and Taylor, *op. cit.*

fundamental questions: (1) What are the desirable objectives of the social work curriculum? (2) What content and educational experiences are needed to attain those educational objectives? (3) What is the most effective organization of content and educational experience in terms of graduate and undergraduate levels of education, curriculum structure, and teaching methods?

Although the curriculum study was carried out as a total enterprise, the project approach was used and these individual projects fell into four major areas:

1. Specific curriculum areas—projects devised to examine the curriculum in the areas of Human Growth and Behavior, the Social Services, and Social Work Practice

2. Selected fields of practice—projects devised to study elements of practice in rehabilitation, public social services, and corrections

3. Undergraduate education for social work

4. Content on social work values and ethics found throughout the curriculum

Each project was planned to identify educational objectives in existing curricula, to formulate a series of desirable objectives, and to review the objectives in the light of educational theory as to the possibility of their being learned effectively in the time and conditions available. The project directors had consultation and assistance from panels of educators and practitioners in social work and related disciplines.

The underlying question for the total study was: What knowledge, attitudes, and skills are needed for effective practice of social work—and in what areas are they needed? Ernest F. Witte notes that the Curriculum Study did not seem to recommend a radical departure from the existing curriculum in schools of social work.

> Rather, it suggests a modification in the time distribution, in objectives, in new constellations of learning experiences, a somewhat different and more clearly defined role for field instruction, and the desirability for a highly integrated curriculum and greater continuity between undergraduate and graduate education for social work. Undoubtedly the most controversial aspect of the report relates to the suggestion that professional education be started in the third year of undergraduate education and that the current second year of graduate study be devoted to a one-year practicum spent in a recognized agency.[10]

[10] Ernest F. Witte, "Education for Social Work," in Russell H. Kurtz, ed., *Social Work Yearbook, 1960* (New York: National Association of Social Workers, 1960), p. 228.

The Curriculum Study was published in fourteen volumes,[11] with a comprehensive presentation of its findings and recommendations given by Werner W. Boehm in Volume I.[12] The study was a most important venture and performed a useful service for social work education, suggesting approaches that were certain to be challenged by some, resisted by many, and provocative for all. Its immediate contribution was this arousing of reaction and interaction, the involving of social work educators and practitioners in searching appraisal of what they are thinking and doing. Perhaps its major long-range contribution will be the identification of new content in the curriculum.

At the heart of the Curriculum Study's recommendations is the proposed undergraduate-graduate continuum which was not a new proposal, the ground having been broken by the Hollis-Taylor report. It requires careful study, since it would substantially shift the structure of social work education. For the organization of content in the undergraduate phase,[13] a structural-functional model was constructed indicating the relationship between basic knowledge areas (for example, the social sciences), basic social work knowledge, and the components of professional social work. The desirable educational objectives in this were then reviewed, being divided into four major content areas: socio-cultural basis of social work, group basis of social work, social work and the social functioning of individuals, and the components of professional social work.

In the two graduate years of the continuum the first year would be essentially academic, including class and field instruction, and the second year would be an agency-based practicum in which the student would be placed full time for the academic year in an agency with the experience having a primarily educational rather than employment focus. This would be followed by three integrative seminars in the summer following the practicum year.

These recommendations warranted—and received—searching consideration by social work educators and practitioners. Within the Council on Social Work Education, the Curriculum Committee carefully studied the proposals and their implications. The House of Delegates, representing the Council's total membership, reviewed the recommendations and committee reports. Faculties of schools of social work discussed the

[11] Werner W. Boehm, *et al., op. cit.*

[12] Werner W. Boehm, *Objectives for the Social Work Curriculum of the Future,* volume I of *The Social Work Curriculum Study* (New York: Council on Social Work Education, 1959).

[13] Herbert Bisno, *The Place of the Undergraduate Curriculum in Social Work Education,* volume II, *ibid.*

Curriculum Study volume by volume. The National Association of Social Workers conducted long-term study of the findings and recommendations, both at the national and local chapter levels. Public and private agencies demonstrated their interest and involvement in these processes.

Three years after the publication of the Curriculum Study, and following the above widespread continuing participation in its review, it seems evident that the major specific recommendations have been set aside in favor of retaining the present two-year graduate program. So far as the undergraduate phase of the continuum is concerned, there remains interest on the part of certain schools and individuals but a crystallization of consensus around the viewpoint that it is not appropriate to begin professional preparation for social work practice below the graduate level.

### UNDERGRADUATE EDUCATION FOR SOCIAL WELFARE

At the same time, a clear outgrowth of the curriculum study has been a sharpening and focusing of interest in undergraduate social welfare education. The Council on Social Work Education added a person to its staff whose responsibility is to offer consultative and advisory services to colleges and universities having or developing a concentration of undergraduate courses in social welfare and relevant to social work. In January 1962 the Council published a guiding statement on undergraduate education relevant to social welfare and to social work education.[14]

> The term "social welfare," as used in this document, refers to a broad gamut of services related to the prevention of social ills and the strengthening of the capacity of people to use their potentialities productively. It includes resources in education, health, economic and social services rendered through a variety of professional disciplines as well as through citizen participation. "Social work," as used in this document, refers to one of these professional disciplines and the services its practitioners provide within the general scope of social welfare.
>
> This statement contains suggested areas of knowledge which might be included in undergraduate programs that provide social welfare content within general and liberal education. The intent of the document is to offer guidance to colleges and universities that wish to improve present programs or offer new programs with social welfare content.
>
> The content suggested here is not prerequisite to admission to graduate professional schools of social work. Graduate schools establish their own

[14] Council on Social Work Education, *Social Welfare Content in Undergraduate Education* (New York: Council on Social Work Education, 1962).

prerequisites for admission, and it is recognized they will continue to admit students with many types of undergraduate education. However, this content would be expected to contribute to the preparation of students for entrance to schools of social work. Future evaluation of experience with a variety of programs of undergraduate preparation will undoubtedly shed light on desirable preprofessional requirements for entry into professional schools.

The profession of social work is currently giving attention to identifying some of the tasks or positions in the social welfare field which could be designated for persons without graduate professional preparation. Pending the resolution of this problem, it is assumed that the content in this document will also provide useful preparation for those positions in social welfare which are now available to college graduates.

Moreover, the significance of social welfare in modern society indicates that the liberal education of all undergraduate students would be enriched by content on social welfare as an institution. Graduates of colleges and universities or responsible citizens and potential community leaders need an informed understanding of the purposes and value of social welfare in a democratic society.[15]

Although the Council serves as the recognized accrediting agency for graduate professional education, it has no accrediting function in undergraduate education. However, through its staff person and other services it does offer to undergraduate departments within its membership consultative and advisory services, publications and technical materials, and opportunities for exchange of views and information. By December 1964 the number of departments and schools in the United States offering a concentration of undergraduate courses recognized by the Council on Social Work Education had grown to 140.

### 1962 CURRICULUM POLICY STATEMENT

The most recent significant development in curriculum planning within the graduate professional schools was the approval by the board of directors of the Council on Social Work Education on October 19, 1962, of a new curriculum policy statement which supersedes previous curriculum policy statements. It spells out in more explicit and clear-cut fashion the educational goals of the general curriculum and of its major components.

The former course sequences identified in the 1952 curriculum policy statement are slightly changed. The curriculum remains developed as

[15] *Ibid.*, pp. 3–4.

a unified whole with three major components: Social Welfare Policy and Services, Human Behavior and the Social Environment, and Methods of Social Work Practice. These categories describe the specified broad areas of content to be covered but do not necessarily delineate curriculum structure.

Social Welfare Policy and Services extends and refocuses the content of the former Social Services sequence, placing more emphasis on social policy and new emphasis on prevention and control as areas of concern for social work. It also distinguishes more clearly between social work as a profession and social welfare as the field in which social work functions. Human Behavior and the Social Environment goes further than the 1952 statement concerning human growth and behavior in making the inclusion of sociocultural material more explicit. Methods of Social Work Practice comprise essentially the content of the former Social Work Practice sequence. It comes out strongly for a class and field concentration in community organization, as well as in casework and group work. Breadth and diversity of field instruction are sought, recognizing that compartmentalization of service and preoccupation with a specific social work method may need to yield to changing societal requirements.

Within the general framework of the total curriculum and its three content areas, the specific ordering of the ways of meeting its objectives is clearly left to the individual school.

### Post-Master's Education

A final development in the evolution of social work education which needs to be mentioned is that of the growing post-master's program. For many years doctoral education in social work was limited to one or two schools. Seventeen schools in the United States and Canada now offer advanced programs leading to a third-year certificate or doctoral degree. It seems clear that social work will look increasingly to the doctoral program for superior competence in teaching, research, supervision, and administration.

*Chapter 3*

# ATTITUDES TOWARD LIBERAL EDUCATION
# AND SOCIAL WORK*

AS ALREADY NOTED IN CHAPTER 2, ONE SEGMENT OF THIS STUDY consisted of a questionnaire polling the opinions of the faculties in social work toward the liberal arts. In order to make the data comparable to other material already collected and analyzed in other professional fields, the same inventory[1] was used.

If social work had been studied separately, a somewhat different questionnaire would have been constructed. Of the ten professional areas studied, only social work education is located primarily at the graduate level. In this sense, education for social work is more nearly comparable to medicine and law than to engineering, nursing, or pharmacy. Of the 116 undergraduate departments studied which prepare students for advanced social work education, ninety-six offer programs which lead to a degree in sociology or psychology. Only eight give undergraduate degrees in the school of social work. Most of the faculty members in the graduate school programs have little knowledge of the undergraduate programs. Their students, more frequently than not, have had their undergraduate work at another institution. Because some of the graduate schools of social work are located in metropolitan centers away from the

*This chapter is a condensation by Mrs. Marlene Miller of an unpublished study, "The Liberal Arts as Viewed by Faculty Members in Home Economics and Social Work," made by Dr. Margaret Lorimer, Office of Institutional Research, Michigan State University.

[1] Paul L. Dressel, Lewis B. Mayhew, and Earl J. McGrath, *The Liberal Arts as Viewed by Faculty Members in Professional Schools.* (New York: Teachers College Press, Teachers College, Columbia University, 1959), pp. 63–68. See also Appendix B, pp. 97–102, *infra.*

main campus, the social work faculty members may have little contact with others in their institutions. Hence, many felt they were not qualified to answer questions bearing either on persons outside their own faculties, or on the prevailing patterns of undergraduate programs.

For these reasons, some parts of the inventory were not relevant to social work, and the results of this study must be interpreted with these limitations in mind. However, items which deal with the attitudes toward liberal arts education, the desired proportion and pattern of the curriculum, and the specific liberal arts courses which should be required were as applicable to social work as to any other professional field.

## THE SAMPLE[2]

### GRADUATE SCHOOL FACULTY

Inventories were mailed to the administrative officers of the fifty-six accredited graduate professional schools of social work in the United States listed by the Council on Social Work Education for distribution to their faculty members. Forty of the fifty-six institutions are represented in the tabulated responses; 476 (64 per cent) inventories of the 744 distributed were returned in time for processing. The rank of the respondents, when compared to the percentage by rank of social work faculty members reported by the Council on Social Work Education,[3] indicates that a fairly representative sample was obtained, varying only in including slightly more instructors and slightly fewer associate professors. Because no data are available on years of service of all social work faculty members, comparisons in this area could not be made. The sample shows over 50 per cent having one to ten years of service. This is to be expected because the sample includes more persons in the lower ranks.

In order to make a more careful study of the attitudes of graduate faculties, the total group was subdivided three ways:

1. by type of institution—public or private;
2. by affiliation with undergraduate programs—a presocial work major in a liberal arts department, an undergraduate degree in social welfare, or no affiliation with a particular undergraduate program;

[2] Tables showing in detail the various characteristics of the three groups were computed by Margaret Lorimer and included in the unpublished study already mentioned.

[3] *Statistics on Social Work Education,* Academic Year, 1960–61, Bulletin No. 62-64-1.

3. by standing or reputation of the graduate school—responses from the faculty of six of the oldest graduate schools were compared with the others.

These divisions revealed the following differences. Respondents from faculties in publicly supported institutions showed a higher proportion (37.3 per cent to 23.8 per cent) holding a doctor's degree. The distributions of faculty ranks were essentially the same, although the public institutions had more research associates and lecturers and fewer instructors than did private institutions. Slightly more of the respondents from private institutions (82.6 per cent to 77.6 per cent) had a bachelor's degree in the liberal arts area. Fifty-five per cent of the respondents had no direct affiliation with undergraduate programs; 19.3 per cent were connected with a department in the college of liberal arts; 25 per cent were affiliated with a department in the school of social work. The third group differed from the other two principally in having a higher proportion of doctor's degrees and a higher proportion of research associates and lecturers among its respondents.

DIRECTORS OF UNDERGRADUATE PREPROFESSIONAL
SOCIAL WELFARE CURRICULA

As of January 1962, the Council on Social Work Education listed 116 undergraduate departments offering courses preparing graduates for advanced professional education or employment in social welfare agencies. Sixty-seven or 57 per cent of the directors of these departments filled out an inventory sent to them.

In comparing the characteristics of the respondents according to type of institution, it was found that the sample was about equally divided between public and private institutions. There was, however, a significant difference in the proportion of master's and doctor's degrees held; more directors in private institutions held degrees in social science while those in public institutions more often held degrees in social work. Since most of the respondents worked in departments with no direct affiliation with a graduate school of social work, it can be assumed that most of them hold membership in liberal arts departments which offer instruction preparatory to graduate study in social work.

PRACTITIONERS

This study also investigated the attitudes of practicing social workers toward the value of their liberal arts education in their professional activities. Of the inventories sent to each president of the 156 local chapters of the National Association of Social Workers, eighty-three (53 per cent) were returned in time for processing.

Data tabulated from the brief questionnaire which accompanied this inventory showed the experiences of the respondents to be extensive and representative of many fields of practice. Of the eighty-three respondents, thirty-five were administrators, twenty were supervisors, fourteen were workers, and fourteen represented multiple responsibilities or other responsibilities. The primary fields of practice were child welfare, family welfare, and psychiatric social work. Eighty-three different communities, varying in size from less than 10,000 to over a million, were represented. The median number of years of experience was from sixteen to twenty years.

The three groups included in the sample differed somewhat in educational backgrounds. The majority of graduate faculty members and practitioners obtained their master's degrees in the field of social work (59.7 per cent and 78.3 per cent, respectively), while, for the undergraduate directors, a larger percentage of master's degrees were in the field of social science (44.8 per cent), with social work a close second (34.3 per cent).

Because of the diversity in these three groups (graduate school faculty members, undergraduate directors, and practitioners), their opinions have been tabulated separately.

### ATTITUDES TOWARD THE LIBERAL ARTS

#### GRADUATE FACULTY MEMBERS

Part I of the ninety-one-item inventory inquired into the attitudes of social work faculty members toward the value of education in liberal arts subjects. These attitudes were explored through the use of twenty-six statements designed to solicit views concerning some of the basic issues which must be faced by those who have responsibility for constructing a curriculum in professional education. The responses of the graduate faculty members in social work are presented in Table 1.

One who reviews these replies must conclude that faculty members in graduate schools of social work generally believe in the value of a liberal arts background for their students. Yet they exhibited some inconsistency and vacillation about a number of matters; for example, the amount of time a student can reasonably be expected or required to devote to liberal arts instruction (Items 3, 4, 24, etc.). These concerns of faculty members about the time to be devoted to preparatory liberal education doubtless spring from an awareness of the pressures for greater

TABLE 1.   PERCENTAGES OF FACULTY MEMBERS OF GRADUATE SCHOOLS OF SOCIAL
WORK EXPRESSING CERTAIN ATTITUDES TOWARD LIBERAL ARTS REQUIREMENTS
(N=476)

| Abbreviated inventory statement | Agree | Disagree | Concerned but undecided | Indifferent |
|---|---|---|---|---|
| 1. All students should be required to take liberal arts courses | 99.1 | 0.4 | 0.2 | — |
| 2. Liberal arts courses should be specifically adapted to needs of technical students | 5.5 | 89.0 | 4.8 | 0.4 |
| 3. More liberal arts courses, even if curriculum must be lengthened | 60.2 | 11.0 | 27.7 | 0.2 |
| 4. In conflict for time, liberal arts requirements should be reduced | 8.6 | 69.6 | 19.8 | 0.4 |
| 5. Liberal arts courses better in developing broad intellectual interests | 80.4 | 8.1 | 9.9 | 1.1 |
| 6. Liberal arts students at disadvantage with those taking specialized work | 9.7 | 78.9 | 10.5 | 0.2 |
| 7. Technically trained people lack imagination and broad perspectives | 81.3 | 5.3 | 12.3 | 0.4 |
| 8. No differences in purposes of liberal and specialized education | 2.4 | 93.2 | 3.1 | 0.7 |
| 9. People with both liberal and specialized education better off vocationally | 82.4 | 4.6 | 11.4 | 1.1 |
| 10. Every professional curriculum should have some liberal arts courses | 77.1 | 11.9 | 9.4 | 0.2 |
| 11. Values of liberal arts unattainable | 3.5 | 85.5 | 7.9 | 1.8 |
| 12. Specialized curricula should have a few electives | 30.1 | 52.3 | 15.4 | 0.7 |
| 13. Professors of liberal arts courses should hold appointment in specialized school | 12.5 | 74.7 | 11.4 | 0.9 |
| 14. Bright technical students will pick up liberal arts experience on their own | 5.9 | 77.6 | 14.3 | 0.9 |
| 15. Liberal values as well achieved through technical courses | 5.3 | 81.9 | 11.4 | 0.7 |

TABLE 1, *Continued*

| Abbreviated inventory statement | Agree | Disagree | Concerned but undecided | Indifferent |
|---|---|---|---|---|
| 16. Specialized courses are best for technical education | 17.4 | 72.9 | 9.0 | 0.2 |
| 17. Combination of liberal arts and specialized courses destroys values of both | 7.0 | 82.4 | 9.7 | 0.2 |
| 18. Liberal arts courses are specialized courses | 20.2 | 62.4 | 12.7 | 2.6 |
| 19. Every post–high school program should offer general education | 87.9 | 2.9 | 7.7 | 1.1 |
| 20. Liberal arts professors penalize students in technical fields | 1.8 | 69.6 | 24.4 | 3.3 |
| 21. Liberal arts degree should be prerequisite for professional curriculum | 52.3 | 23.1 | 23.5 | 0.7 |
| 22. Liberal education should be postponed for adult education | 1.3 | 97.3 | 0.9 | — |
| 23. Students now required to take excessive amount of liberal arts work | 2.0 | 96.4 | 1.1 | — |
| 24. Students should take more liberal arts courses | 37.3 | 45.0 | 16.0 | 0.4 |
| 25. Students with heavy liberal arts emphasis are poorer employment prospects | 3.3 | 85.7 | 8.3 | 1.1 |
| 26. Students should meet liberal arts requirement with courses related to specialty | 11.2 | 80.4 | 6.4 | 0.4 |

specialization and for more specialized training than can be offered in the time allotted to professional training, of the great need for social workers, and of the impatience of young people to start their careers. This conflict between the desire for greater breadth and for professional specialization appears in the fact that a large percentage of the respondents expressed a belief in the value of a strong background in the liberal arts— preferably a degree in social science—and elsewhere demonstrated considerable pride in the fact that training for this profession is nearly all on the graduate level, and yet only 52 per cent agreed that a liberal arts degree should be required for admission to a professional school (Item 21), and an additional 23.5 per cent expressed concern or indecision. On the other hand, they believed that liberal education should not be postponed for adult education, and that a bright technical student would not pick up liberal arts experience on his own.

In additional tables compiled by Margaret Lorimer, but not reproduced here, the responses from the graduate faculty members were broken down into the previously mentioned subgroups. Only a few of the more significant differences will be mentioned here. Sixty-two per cent of the graduate faculty members in private institutions but only 41 per cent of those in public institutions believed a liberal arts degree should be prerequisite to professional study. The faculty members of private institutions apparently are more likely to view liberal arts and professional training as separate rather than concurrent phases of a student's education. About 83 per cent of those in public institutions would include liberal arts courses in professional curricula as compared to 71 per cent in private institutions. Another difference appears in the fact that about 53 per cent of those in public institutions disagreed but only 38 per cent in the private institutions disagreed with the statement that students should take *more* liberal arts courses, while an additional 21 per cent in the latter were concerned but undecided.

More faculty members in the selected group of graduate schools would make the liberal arts degree prerequisite. Throughout their responses, faculty members from these selected institutions tended to place a higher value on liberal arts than their colleagues elsewhere. This attitude appears also in the belief of those in public institutions that liberal values might be achieved as well from professional courses as from liberal arts courses and that liberal arts were specialized courses.

The attitudes of the graduate faculty group and of each of the subgroups toward the value of liberal arts courses are exhibited in Table 2 in which an index was obtained by scoring each respondent's questionnaire according to the favorable responses checked. The meaning of these figures can be inferred from their relationship to 26.0 which would be a completely favorable score.

DIRECTORS OF UNDERGRADUATE SOCIAL WELFARE PROGRAMS

Like the graduate faculty members, the directors of undergraduate programs of social welfare strongly endorsed liberal arts requirements and reiterated the importance of a strong background of liberal arts as preparation for social workers. Table 3, which presents the "agree," "disagree," and "concerned but undecided" responses, shows that the differences between the attitudes of graduate faculty members and directors of undergraduate programs are small. If the views of only the grad-

TABLE 2. INDEX OF FAVORABLE ATTITUDES OF GRADUATE SCHOOL FACULTY
MEMBERS TOWARD THE LIBERAL ARTS REQUIREMENTS

| Group | Index |
|---|---|
| Total Group (N=476) | 20.1 |
| Subgroups: | |
| Public institutions (N=218) | 19.9 |
| Private institutions (N=237) | 23.3 |
| Selected institutions (N=120) | 20.7 |
| Other institutions (N=356) | 19.9 |
| Affiliation with a liberal arts department (N=92) | 19.5 |
| Affiliation with an undergraduate professional school (N=119) | 20.3 |
| No affiliation with an undergraduate program (N=265) | 20.4 |
| Academic Rank: | |
| Dean (N=20) | 20.9 |
| Department head (N=19) | 19.3 |
| Professor (N=36) | 20.7 |
| Associate professor (N=130) | 19.9 |
| Assistant professor (N=125) | 20.1 |
| Instructor (N=45) | 18.8 |
| Other (N=40) | 19.9 |

uate faculty members in the top ranks are used in the comparison, these differences are even smaller.

When the undergraduate directors are divided into public and private groups the latter were much more likely than the former to agree that liberal arts courses better develop broad intellectual interests, that liberal arts degrees should be prerequisite for a professional curriculum, and that students should take more liberal arts courses. More of the undergraduate directors in public than in private institutions agreed that liberal arts values are achieved as well through professional courses, and the same pattern held in respect to the view that specialized courses are best for professional education.

Undergraduate directors in institutions which have a graduate program of social work are somewhat less favorable toward the liberal arts than those with no affiliation. The difference is too small to emphasize, but if an explanation were to be provided, it might be that those institutions having both undergraduate and graduate programs are usually large, complex universities where the image of the liberal arts is less "liberal" than that found in the smaller colleges which offer a presocial work curriculum.

TABLE 3.  Percentages of Directors of Undergraduate Programs in Social Work Expressing Certain Attitudes toward Liberal Arts Requirements (N=67)

| Abbreviated inventory statement | Agree | Disagree | Concerned but undecided |
|---|---|---|---|
| 1. All students should be required to take liberal arts courses | 98.5 | 1.5 | — |
| 2. Liberal arts courses should be specifically adapted to needs of technical students | 6.0 | 86.5 | 7.5 |
| 3. More liberal arts courses, even if curriculum must be lengthened | 67.1 | 7.5 | 23.9 |
| 4. In conflict for time, liberal arts requirements should be reduced | 7.5 | 76.0 | 16.4 |
| 5. Liberal arts courses better in developing broad intellectual interests | 83.5 | 7.5 | 9.0 |
| 6. Liberal arts students at disadvantage with those taking specialized work | 19.4 | 62.7 | 17.9 |
| 7. Technically trained people lack imagination and broad perspectives | 80.6 | 7.5 | 10.4 |
| 8. No differences in purposes of liberal and specialized education | — | 94.0 | 4.5 |
| 9. People with both liberal and specialized education better off vocationally | 83.5 | 6.0 | 9.0 |
| 10. Every professional curriculum should have some liberal arts courses | 94.0 | 3.0 | 3.0 |
| 11. Values of liberal arts unattainable | 1.5 | 82.1 | 14.9 |
| 12. Specialized curricula should have a few electives | 30.0 | 55.2 | 11.9 |
| 13. Professors of liberal arts courses should hold appointment in specialized school | 7.5 | 83.6 | 4.5 |
| 14. Bright technical students will pick up liberal arts experience on their own | 7.5 | 83.6 | 7.5 |
| 15. Liberal values as well achieved through technical courses | 10.4 | 74.6 | 13.4 |
| 16. Specialized courses are best for technical education | 16.4 | 74.6 | 9.0 |

TABLE 3, *Continued*

| Abbreviated inventory statement | Agree | Disagree | Concerned but undecided |
|---|---|---|---|
| 17. Combination of liberal arts and specialized courses destroys values of both | 4.5 | 94.0 | 1.5 |
| 18. Liberal arts courses are specialized courses | 17.9 | 64.1 | 17.9 |
| 19. Every post–high school program should offer general education | 88.1 | 1.5 | 10.4 |
| 20. Liberal arts professors penalize students in technical fields | 3.0 | 74.6 | 19.4 |
| 21. Liberal arts degree should be prerequisite for professional curriculum | 55.2 | 26.9 | 16.4 |
| 22. Liberal education should be postponed for adult education | 1.5 | 97.0 | 1.5 |
| 23. Students now required to take excessive amount of liberal arts work | 4.5 | 92.5 | 3.0 |
| 24. Students should take more liberal arts courses | 25.4 | 62.7 | 10.4 |
| 25. Students with heavy liberal arts emphasis are poorer employment prospects | 10.4 | 79.1 | 11.9 |
| 26. Students should meet liberal arts requirements with courses related to specialty | 13.4 | 79.1 | 4.5 |

Table 4, which summarizes the favorable attitudes expressed by directors of undergraduate programs according to the two subgroups, shows that the differences are not very significant.

PRACTITIONERS

Table 5 presents information gained from practicing social workers. This group of professionals also endorsed the liberal arts requirements as they now understand them and as they looked back on their own undergraduate experiences.

Perhaps the most striking difference between the three groups under study is the fact that more than 15 per cent of the practitioner group expressed concern but indecision about eleven of the twenty-six statements. This compares to six such statements for the graduate faculty group and the undergraduate directors. The practitioners expressed the greatest

TABLE 4.   INDEX OF FAVORABLE ATTITUDES TOWARD THE LIBERAL ARTS
EXPRESSED BY DIRECTORS OF UNDERGRADUATE PROGRAMS OF SOCIAL WORK

| Group | Index[a] |
|---|---|
| Total Group (N=67) | 19.4 |
| Subgroups: | |
| Public institutions (N=31) | 18.8 |
| Private institutions (N=36) | 19.9 |
| Affiliated with a graduate program (N=8) | 19.3 |
| Not affiliated with a graduate program (N=59) | 20.4 |

[a] Perfect score: 26.0

concern about the time involved in obtaining a liberal arts background and adequate professional training. Statements which suggest longer preparation for graduate work and those which question the value of graduate work evoked this concern. Undoubtedly, the practitioners felt the need for both kinds of training, but were concerned about the time required to accomplish both goals.

Using the same attitudinal index in summarizing the responses for the practitioners, a score of 19.3 was obtained, which is essentially the same as the 19.4 reported in Table 4 for graduate faculty and undergraduate directors.

Table 6 shows a comparison of the attitudes of faculty members in social work programs with the attitudes of faculty members in nine other professions. These figures clearly indicate that the attitudes of social work faculty members are more favorable than any others. An especially favorable attitude toward liberal arts preparation is revealed among the graduate faculty in selected schools of social work.

## MEANS OF PROVIDING LIBERAL ARTS EDUCATION TO SOCIAL WORK MAJORS

### PROPORTION

Part II of the inventory deals with a very significant aspect of the total educational preparation of social workers; namely, the proportion of the total undergraduate program to be devoted to liberal arts courses. Table 7 indicates the preferred percentages of the three sample groups and their subdivisions.

Graduate faculty members, as a group, appear to be unanimously in favor of the "over 50%" classification. Differences of opinion occur

TABLE 5. PERCENTAGES OF SOCIAL WORK PRACTITIONERS EXPRESSING CERTAIN ATTITUDES TOWARD LIBERAL ARTS REQUIREMENTS IN UNDERGRADUATE PROGRAMS (N=83)

| Abbreviated inventory statement | Agree | Disagree | Concerned but undecided |
|---|---|---|---|
| 1. All students should be required to take liberal arts courses | 100.0 | — | — |
| 2. Liberal arts courses should be specifically adapted to needs of technical students | 14.5 | 77.1 | 8.4 |
| 3. More liberal arts courses, even if curriculum must be lengthened | 53.0 | 14.5 | 31.8 |
| 4. In conflict for time, liberal arts requirements should be reduced | 9.6 | 55.4 | 33.3 |
| 5. Liberal arts courses better in developing broad intellectual interests. | 90.4 | 3.6 | 5.1 |
| 6. Liberal arts students at disadvantage with those taking specialized work | 15.7 | 68.7 | 15.8 |
| 7. Technically trained people lack imagination and broad perspectives | 81.9 | 4.8 | 14.0 |
| 8. No differences in purposes of liberal and specialized education | — | 97.6 | 1.2 |
| 9. People with both liberal and specialized education better off vocationally | 86.9 | 3.6 | 9.9 |
| 10. Every professional curriculum should have some liberal arts courses | 84.4 | 4.8 | 9.9 |
| 11. Values of liberal arts unattainable | 1.2 | 84.4 | 13.7 |
| 12. Specialized curricula should have a few electives | 22.9 | 60.3 | 16.4 |
| 13. Professors of liberal arts courses should hold appointment in specialized school | 4.8 | 79.5 | 9.9 |
| 14. Bright technical students will pick up liberal arts experience on their own | 3.6 | 80.7 | 16.4 |
| 15. Liberal values as well achieved through technical courses | 7.2 | 66.3 | 24.5 |
| 16. Specialized courses are best for technical education | 18.1 | 65.1 | 17.4 |

TABLE 5, *Continued*

| Abbreviated inventory statement | Agree | Disagree | Concerned but undecided |
|---|---|---|---|
| 17. Combination of liberal arts and specialized courses destroys values of both | 3.6 | 89.2 | 7.6 |
| 18. Liberal arts courses are specialized courses | 24.1 | 51.8 | 23.5 |
| 19. Every post–high school program should offer general education | 88.0 | 3.6 | 7.7 |
| 20. Liberal arts professors penalize students in technical fields | — | 70.0 | 6.8 |
| 21. Liberal arts degree should be prerequisite for professional curriculum | 43.4 | 31.3 | 26.1 |
| 22. Liberal education should be postponed for adult education | 1.2 | 96.4 | 1.2 |
| 23. Students now required to take excessive amount of liberal arts work | 2.4 | 90.4 | 4.9 |
| 24. Students should take more liberal arts courses | 24.1 | 43.4 | 32.2 |
| 25. Students with heavy liberal arts emphasis are poorer employment prospects | 10.8 | 67.5 | 19.5 |
| 26. Students should meet liberal arts requirements with courses related to specialty | 24.1 | 60.3 | 13.7 |

when subdivided by rank with deans and department heads at 78.9 and 77.8 per cent, respectively, for "over 50%," while assistant professors and instructors state a preference for 44.5 per cent, respectively. Relatively few of the graduate faculty members would have allotted less than 36 per cent to the liberal arts category.

The responses of the directors of undergraduate programs do not differ significantly from the total group, but when compared with the corresponding graduate faculty rank, differences appear. As indicated, nearly 80 per cent of the graduate school deans and department heads favored more than 50 per cent of the undergraduate program in the liberal arts, whereas only 50 per cent of the undergraduate directors would require this much. Obviously, and not unnaturally, the directors of undergraduate social welfare programs were less willing to reduce the under-

TABLE 6.  INDEX OF FAVORABLE ATTITUDES TOWARD THE LIBERAL ARTS
EXPRESSED BY FACULTY MEMBERS IN THE VARIOUS PROFESSIONAL AREAS[a]

| Area | Index[b] |
|---|---|
| Social work: graduate faculty (N=476) | 20.1 |
| Social work: undergraduate faculty (N=67) | 19.4 |
| Social work: graduate faculty in selected outstanding institutions (N=120) | 20.7 |
| Nursing (N=318) | 19.3 |
| Journalism (N=201) | 19.0 |
| Business (N=277) | 18.4 |
| Education (N=582) | 18.4 |
| Pharmacy (N=96) | 17.5 |
| Agriculture (N=824) | 16.8 |
| Home economics:[c] total group (N=181) | 16.7 |
| Engineering (N=595) | 16.2 |
| Music (N=351) | 16.2 |

[a] Paul L. Dressel, Lewis B. Mayhew, and Earl J. McGrath. *The Liberal Arts as Viewed by Faculty Members in Professional Schools, op. cit.,* p. 14.
[b] Index based on 26-item questionnaire.
[c] Home economics number of individuals was expanded in the unpublished study by Margaret Lorimer.

graduate professional component than were the senior graduate faculty members.

The preferences of practitioners more nearly agreed with those of the undergraduate directors than with the graduate school faculty members, but the administrators among the practitioners would require the most work in the liberal arts subjects. These are very significant findings which the profession as a whole should contemplate in terms of the general policy of favoring a graduate education as the primary and strongly preferred preparation for professional practice. These figures suggest that those students who begin their professional education even at an elementary level in the undergraduate years will, if they are guided by the subject-matter preferences of the undergraduate directors, have a narrower range of intellectual experiences than their counterparts who attended an institution with no professional undergraduate work. If the views of the graduate faculties have any validity they ought to be brought home more vigorously and cogently to the heads of undergraduate departments. The data presented later in Chapter 4 will show that as far as the undergraduate patterns of courses are concerned there is no "best" preparation for graduate social work. Hence the graduate faculties do not seem to be handicapping prospective graduate students in this field by urging a broad preparatory liberal education.

TABLE 7.  PERCENTAGES OF GRADUATE SCHOOL FACULTY, DIRECTORS OF UNDER-
GRADUATE PROGRAMS, AND PRACTITIONERS RECOMMENDING VARIOUS PORTIONS OF
TOTAL UNDERGRADUATE PROGRAM TO BE DEVOTED TO LIBERAL ARTS (*Item* 31)

| Group | 1–10% | 11–25% | 26–35% | 36–50% | Over 50% |
|---|---|---|---|---|---|
| GRADUATE FACULTY | 2.6 | 4.2 | 9.6 | 24.8 | 56.7 |
| Subgroups: | | | | | |
| Public institutions | 4.1 | 5.0 | 10.6 | 26.1 | 51.8 |
| Private institutions | 1.3 | 3.4 | 8.9 | 23.6 | 61.6 |
| Selected institutions | .8 | .8 | 11.7 | 20.8 | 65.0 |
| Other institutions | 3.3 | 5.4 | 8.9 | 26.3 | 54.0 |
| Department of liberal arts | 4.7 | 5.9 | 8.3 | 29.8 | 50.0 |
| Department of professional school | 5.0 | 3.4 | 10.1 | 31.9 | 48.8 |
| No affiliation | .8 | 3.9 | 9.9 | 19.8 | 62.8 |
| Deans | — | 5.3 | — | 15.8 | 78.9 |
| Department heads | — | 5.6 | — | 16.7 | 77.8 |
| Professors | 3.5 | 3.5 | 5.9 | 12.9 | 72.9 |
| Associate professors | 2.5 | 5.0 | 5.0 | 25.6 | 59.5 |
| Assistant professors | 1.7 | 3.4 | 14.3 | 33.6 | 44.5 |
| Instructors | 6.6 | 4.4 | 13.3 | 31.1 | 42.2 |
| Others | 2.6 | 5.1 | 17.9 | 23.1 | 51.3 |
| UNDERGRADUATE DIRECTORS | 1.5 | 7.5 | 11.9 | 23.9 | 49.2 |
| Subgroups: | | | | | |
| Public institutions | — | 9.7 | 12.9 | 25.8 | 41.9 |
| Private institutions | 2.8 | 5.6 | 11.1 | 22.2 | 55.5 |
| Graduate school affiliation | — | 12.5 | 12.5 | 25.0 | 50.0 |
| No graduate school affiliation | 1.7 | 6.8 | 11.8 | 23.7 | 49.2 |
| PRACTITIONERS | 1.2 | 7.2 | 14.4 | 37.3 | 39.7 |
| Subgroups: | | | | | |
| Workers | — | — | 21.4 | 42.9 | 35.7 |
| Supervisors | 5.0 | 10.0 | 5.0 | 55.0 | 25.0 |
| Administrators | — | 8.6 | 20.0 | 28.6 | 42.9 |
| Teachers | — | 16.7 | — | 66.6 | 16.7 |
| Multiple responsibilities | 1.2 | 7.2 | 14.4 | 37.3 | 39.7 |

PATTERNS PREFERRED

Part II of the inventory also asked respondents to indicate their preferences among five patterns for placing liberal arts instruction in the
sequence of years devoted to preparation for professional employment.
The options were: (1) placing all liberal arts courses in the first two

TABLE 8.   PERCENTAGES OF GRADUATE SCHOOL FACULTY, DIRECTORS OF
UNDERGRADUATE PROGRAMS, AND PRACTITIONERS PREFERRING CERTAIN PATTERNS
FOR OFFERING REQUIRED LIBERAL ARTS COURSES (*Item* 32)

| Group | First two years | Evenly over four years | Most in first year then decreasing | Senior year | Conven- ience |
|---|---|---|---|---|---|
| GRADUATE FACULTY | 3.9 | 68.8 | 21.1 | .9 | 3.3 |
| Subgroups: | | | | | |
| Public institutions | 5.5 | 61.5 | 28.0 | .5 | 3.7 |
| Private institutions | 2.5 | 75.9 | 14.8 | 1.3 | 3.0 |
| Selected institutions | 5.8 | 68.3 | 18.3 | .8 | 3.3 |
| Other institutions | 3.3 | 69.3 | 22.1 | .9 | 3.3 |
| Department of liberal arts | 3.6 | 72.6 | 16.6 | — | 5.9 |
| Department of profession- al school | 8.4 | 55.5 | 31.9 | .8 | 3.4 |
| No affiliation | 2.0 | 73.9 | 17.4 | 1.2 | 2.4 |
| Deans | 5.3 | 68.4 | 15.8 | — | — |
| Department heads | — | 66.7 | 27.8 | — | 5.6 |
| Professors | 3.5 | 74.1 | 17.6 | 1.2 | 2.4 |
| Associate professors | 3.3 | 73.6 | 17.4 | 1.7 | 2.5 |
| Assistant professors | 4.2 | 61.3 | 28.6 | — | 4.2 |
| Instructors | 4.4 | 73.3 | 17.8 | 2.2 | — |
| Others | 7.7 | 64.1 | 23.1 | — | 5.1 |
| UNDERGRADUATE DIRECTORS | 1.3 | 55.2 | 35.8 | — | 6.0 |
| Subgroups: | | | | | |
| Public institutions | 3.2 | 54.8 | 33.2 | — | — |
| Private institutions | — | 55.5 | 38.9 | — | 2.8 |
| Graduate school affilia- tion | 12.5 | 62.5 | 12.5 | — | 12.5 |
| No graduate school affiliation | — | 54.2 | 39.0 | — | 5.1 |
| PRACTITIONERS | 8.4 | 56.6 | 32.5 | — | 2.4 |
| Subgroups: | | | | | |
| Workers | 7.1 | 57.1 | 35.7 | — | — |
| Supervisors | 10.0 | 65.0 | 20.0 | — | 5.0 |
| Administrators | 5.7 | 54.3 | 37.1 | — | 2.9 |
| Teachers | 20.0 | 40.0 | 40.0 | — | — |
| Multiple responsibili- ties | 16.7 | 66.6 | 16.7 | — | 2.4 |

years; (2) spreading liberal arts requirements over the four years; (3) requiring most of the liberal arts courses in the first year and decreasing the
amount thereafter; (4) requiring most of the liberal arts instruction in the
senior year; and (5) offering these courses at any time convenient to the

TABLE 9.  PERCENTAGES OF GRADUATE SCHOOL FACULTY, DIRECTORS OF
UNDERGRADUATE PROGRAMS, AND PRACTITIONERS RECOMMENDING MEANS OF
ENSURING ADEQUATE LIBERAL ARTS COMPONENT (*Item* 33)

| Group | Limited core | Additional year, summer | Extra work | Indepen-dent work | Heavy first two years |
|---|---|---|---|---|---|
| GRADUATE FACULTY | 39.9 | 9.6 | .9 | 1.3 | 43.6 |
| Subgroups: | | | | | |
| Public institutions | 40.4 | 9.6 | .5 | .5 | 47.2 |
| Private institutions | 39.7 | 9.7 | 1.3 | 2.1 | 40.5 |
| Selected institutions | 32.5 | 11.7 | .8 | 2.5 | 44.2 |
| Other institutions | 47.7 | 8.9 | .9 | .9 | 43.6 |
| Department of liberal arts | 48.8 | 10.7 | — | 2.4 | 34.5 |
| Department of profession-al school | 32.8 | 8.4 | .8 | .8 | 54.6 |
| No affiliation | 40.3 | 9.5 | 1.2 | 1.2 | 41.5 |
| Deans | 42.1 | 10.5 | — | — | 36.8 |
| Department heads | 38.9 | 5.6 | — | — | 11.8 |
| Professors | 34.1 | 12.9 | — | 2.4 | 44.7 |
| Associate professors | 40.0 | 11.6 | .8 | 1.7 | 40.5 |
| Assistant professors | 41.2 | 5.9 | .8 | .8 | 47.1 |
| Instructors | 44.4 | 8.9 | 2.2 | — | 44.4 |
| Others | 38.5 | 10.3 | 2.6 | — | 46.2 |
| UNDERGRADUATE DIRECTORS | 34.3 | 13.4 | — | — | 50.7 |
| Subgroups: | | | | | |
| Public institutions | 38.7 | — | — | — | 58.1 |
| Private institutions | 30.5 | 25.0 | — | — | 44.4 |
| Graduate school affilia-tion | 37.5 | 25.0 | — | — | 37.5 |
| No graduate school affiliation | 33.8 | 11.8 | — | — | 52.5 |
| PRACTITIONERS | 49.4 | 3.6 | — | — | 45.8 |
| Subgroups: | | | | | |
| Workers | 35.7 | 7.1 | — | — | 57.1 |
| Supervisors | 45.0 | 10.0 | — | — | 45.0 |
| Administrators | 62.9 | — | — | — | 37.1 |
| Teachers | 40.0 | — | — | — | 60.0 |
| Multiple responsibili-ties | 50.0 | — | — | — | 33.3 |

student. Table 8 contains the breakdown of the responses to this part of the questionnaire.

Graduate school faculty members clearly preferred to spread courses in the liberal arts over the four undergraduate years, and this view was more prevalent in private than in public institutions. Faculty members in graduate schools affiliated with an undergraduate social welfare department also expressed this preference, but inclined more toward requiring most liberal arts courses in the first year, decreasing the amount thereafter. Directors of undergraduate programs in social welfare and practitioners also agreed on the four-year spread of the liberal arts.

MEANS OF ENSURING AN ADEQUATE LIBERAL ARTS COMPONENT

As Table 9 indicates, Part II of the inventory also offered five alternatives for maximizing the liberal arts component of a degree program as follows: (1) a limited core of required courses; (2) an additional year or summer for liberal arts; (3) ample extracurricular opportunities; (4) opportunities for self-education; and (5) two years of heavy liberal arts requirements prior to professional training.

These figures show that faculty members in graduate schools of social work were about equally divided between a limited core of courses and a heavy program of liberal arts in the first two years. Those associated with institutions with an undergraduate social welfare department preferred the two-year concentration. Academic rank did not seem to influence the opinion.

Directors of undergraduate programs leaned somewhat more heavily toward the two-year concentration. One-fourth of those in private institutions and one-fourth of those directly affiliated with a graduate school advocated an additional summer or year to provide more time for liberal studies.

Practitioners were about equally divided between the two plans preferred by faculty members. Administrators again favored liberal arts throughout the four years.

COURSES PREFERRED FOR LIBERAL ARTS REQUIREMENT

Table 10 contains very significant information about the preferences of various groups for the specific liberal arts courses which should be required in eighteen subject areas. Respondents were asked to indicate: (1) courses which should be required of all students; (2) courses which should be optional but encouraged for all students; (3) courses which should be completely optional; (4) courses which students should be discouraged from taking; and (5) courses which students should not be allowed to take except beyond the requirements.

The outstanding preferences for English, the social sciences, and history, literature, and philosophy are obvious in Table 10. The sciences (biology, mathematics, physiology, physics, and chemistry) appear to have a comparatively lower value. The subject-matter preferences of the three groups differ but little except that fewer of the graduate faculty members would require religion; more of the practitioners would require

TABLE 10.  Percentages of Faculty Members in Graduate Schools of Social Work, Directors of Undergraduate Programs in Social Work, and Practitioners in Social Work Recommending That Courses in Each of the Subject-Matter Areas Be Required

| Subject area | Graduate faculty | Directors of undergraduate programs | Practitioners |
|---|---|---|---|
| English | 97.2 | 94.0 | 94.9 |
| Sociology | 90.2 | 97.0 | 91.4 |
| Psychology | 87.5 | 86.5 | 93.9 |
| History | 78.6 | 76.8 | 76.8 |
| Economics | 77.1 | 77.6 | 89.0 |
| Political science | 72.5 | 73.1 | 74.4 |
| Literature | 67.7 | 64.2 | 65.8 |
| Philosophy | 61.3 | 58.2 | 67.0 |
| Biology | 49.5 | 58.2 | 48.8 |
| Mathematics | 35.7 | 49.2 | 32.9 |
| Foreign language | 32.4 | 34.3 | 28.0 |
| Physiology | 29.3 | 22.4 | 40.2 |
| Speech | 20.8 | 26.9 | 45.1 |
| Religion | 11.6 | 28.3 | 25.6 |
| Physics | 8.8 | 7.5 | 14.6 |
| Art | 7.9 | 13.4 | 15.8 |
| Chemistry | 7.0 | 6.0 | 15.8 |
| Music | 5.3 | 7.5 | 9.8 |

50%

physiology and speech, and more of the undergraduate directors would require biology and mathematics.

Two facts shown in Table 10 merit comment. As in all the other professions studied, the members lay the greatest stress on instruction which cultivates competence in the use of the mother tongue. Secondly, like the other professions, social workers, even though they favor broad preparation in the liberal arts fields, tend to place professionally related instruction higher on the list than nonrelated courses. Hence, pharmacists favor biology and chemistry; engineers, science and mathematics; and nurses, the biological sciences. The social workers favor sociology, psychology, history, economics, and political science, in that order, after English. Such subjects as chemistry, physics, and art, only remotely related to the practice of social work, receive little support. The question may be raised, therefore, whether the desire for a "broad" liberal education is really as strong as represented earlier. Ought not social workers know more about the implications of developments in modern science? This study only raises this and related questions; it does not presume to answer them, but the profession cannot fail to face these decisions.

## ATTITUDES AT VARIOUS INSTITUTIONS IN REGARD TO LIBERAL ARTS REQUIREMENTS

### VALUE OF LIBERAL ARTS IN RELATION TO TECHNICAL PROFESSIONAL COURSES

To obtain a measure of institutional atmosphere respondents were asked to indicate what value certain persons or groups among their colleagues placed on the liberal arts in relation to that placed on technical/professional courses. Since this response required an evaluation of the thinking of other persons or groups, faculty members (especially those in graduate schools independent of any specific undergraduate department) were reluctant to comply. Those who did respond, both in the undergraduate and graduate groups, however, believed that the president, the liberal arts administrators, and the faculty members would require more liberal arts courses even at the expense of professional courses. This evaluation is substantiated by actual interviews discussed in Chapter 6. About half of each group believed that social work department heads and faculty members placed the value of liberal arts either equal to or above the value of professional courses. When expressing their own personal views, faculty members were inclined to believe more liberal arts should be required.

### METHODS OF PROVIDING FOR LIBERAL ARTS COURSES

Respondents were asked to indicate the curricular arrangements or policies they thought their colleagues would favor for providing liberal arts courses. Five alternatives were offered: (1) no provision except for well-taught specialized courses; (2) a prescribed set of courses having direct relevance to the specialized field; (3) a few broad courses required of all students and designed to acquaint students with the major areas of the liberal arts; (4) free election of courses from within three or four areas in the liberal arts; and (5) free election from any scheduled liberal arts courses. Because this section of the inventory also required some assumptions about the views of other persons many faculty members, especially in the graduate schools, did not respond. About half of the responding undergraduate directors thought their colleagues, both in their own departments and in the liberal arts departments, preferred free election from three or four liberal arts areas. About one-fourth of them thought their colleagues preferred a prescribed set of courses directly related to social work. When indicating their own preferences, many graduate faculty members preferred a prescribed set of courses related to social work but, at the same time, saw few of their colleagues as favorable to this pattern. The percentage of undergraduate directors preferring the broad courses was much larger than that (52 per cent to less than 15 per cent) of their colleagues whom they adjudged favorable to this pattern.

The responses given to this part of the inventory lead to the conclusion that considerable support exists among both graduate faculties and directors of undergraduate programs for providing a common basic education in the major liberal arts areas rather than depending on free election within the same areas. These responses suggest the prevalence of a view that election has failed to give adequate breadth and that courses elected have perhaps been so highly specialized as to make an adequate background impossible.

PREVAILING ATTITUDES TOWARD LIBERAL ARTS
IN THE RESPONDENT'S OWN INSTITUTION

In the final part of the inventory the respondents were asked to make four evaluations in terms of the following statements: (1) liberal arts courses are typically just another kind of specialized education; (2) liberal arts courses seem to be genuinely attempting to provide a broad education for students not majoring in those fields; (3) liberal arts courses for undergraduates are markedly under the domination of the graduate faculty in those fields, and, finally, (4) technical and professional students are inclined to feel inferior to other students in their liberal arts courses. The respondents were to judge whether these statements were descriptive of the situation at their own university or college. Naturally, practitioners were not in a position to fill in this part of the questionnaire.

Over one-half of the graduate faculties and more than two-thirds of the undergraduate directors responding thought that the liberal arts are *not* just another kind of specialized education. About the same number thought that the liberal arts courses are genuinely planned to give a broad education. About one-third of the graduate faculty and 8 per cent of the undergraduate directors thought that liberal arts courses were *not* under the domination of graduate faculties. Many graduate faculty members withheld judgment.

SUMMARY

Three groups of persons closely associated with social work education—faculty members teaching in graduate schools of social work, directors of undergraduate programs of social welfare, and practitioners who are using their social work education in carrying out their various responsibilities—indicated in their responses to a 91-item inventory that they considered a broad background in the liberal arts as extremely important in their profession.

The attitudes of the two groups of educators, and of practitioners as well, were more favorable toward the liberal arts than those of faculty members in any one of the nine other professional areas, including the related areas of nursing and education. Graduate faculty members generally, and those in the group of selected schools especially, were consistently more favorable to liberal education than the other groups throughout the questionnaire. As found in other professional groups, social work administrators and senior faculty members were more favorable (in that order) to the liberal arts than were their junior colleagues.

Social work faculty members would require a larger percentage of the total degree program to be taken in the liberal arts and would require work in more of the related subject-matter areas than would those in any other professional field. Although they preferred that liberal arts courses be spread throughout the four years of undergraduate work, they favored a few broad courses in each of the liberal arts areas to a free election within the same areas. They tended to place greater value in liberal arts courses in the undergraduate years than in technical/professional courses offered for prospective social workers. On the whole, the social work administrators, faculty members, and practitioners strongly endorsed the liberal arts as a valuable background for professional study.

*Chapter 4*

# THE RELATIONSHIPS BETWEEN UNDERGRADUATE
# PREPARATION AND PERFORMANCE
# IN GRADUATE SCHOOL

EARLIER STUDIES IN THIS SERIES OF INQUIRIES INTO EDUCATION FOR THE practice of the professions revealed a common process of evolution from apprenticeship under an established practitioner to an extended professional educational program, superimposed on varying amounts of preparatory instruction in the liberal arts and sciences.[1] Education in the medical profession exemplifies these developments more clearly than any other. Even as late as 1900 in some states a young man with only a high school education, or even less, could gain admission to medical practice by serving an apprenticeship of several years with a practicing physician. In some states, however, medical schools had been firmly established by the turn of the century, and a few had already urged, if not required, two or more years of premedical education in a liberal arts college. Now the latter requirement has become general and more than three-quarters of those who enter a medical school have already received the bachelor's degree. The requirements in other professions, law, dentistry, and the ministry, for example, though less extensive than in medicine, all exhibit the same trend. Each occupational group at the professional level has recognized that a practitioner can remain competent neither as a worker nor as a citizen in our complex society with only technical preparation for his calling.

As a formally organized occupational group with specific profes-

[1] For a fuller treatment of the stages of development of professional education, see *Liberal Education in the Professions* by Earl J. McGrath (New York: Teachers College Press, Teachers College, Columbia University, 1959).

sional responsibilities social workers constitute a comparatively young profession. It is not surprising, therefore, that this occupational group should have passed very quickly from apprenticeship training to graduate study as proper preparation for professional positions in social work. With the onset of the depression in the 1930's, and the consequent need for a large corps of qualified persons to provide the rapidly expanded services of social welfare, the members of the profession met pressing problems of recruitment and training for immediate employment. In spite of the exigencies of those critical days thoughtful consideration was consistently given to the type of basic education, both general and specialized, that members of the profession were going to need for the effective discharge of their duties as social workers and as citizens. The discussions which began over a quarter century ago, and continue today, exhibit a continuing concern among social work educators for the broad, liberal education of their future professional associates.[2] The profession has not been unanimous in its views on curricular policies and practices, but the weight of opinion has been that

> Before the student learns about social work *per se,* he should learn about the world he lives in, the society he belongs to, the groups of which he is a member and the kind of person he is. In brief, he needs basic knowledge about the universe and his place in it, acquired as part of the general education process of liberal education.[3]

The imposition of such a requirement in presocial work education raises certain questions concerning the amount and kind of instruction which those who contemplate a career in this field should include in their undergraduate years. Should the future graduate student in a school of social work concentrate heavily in sociology in his college experience? Or should he pursue a broad program of studies in the various social sciences? Or should he simply allow his own immediate intellectual interests to guide his choice of subjects and major in any field, even in a discipline as remote from the practice of social work as physics or chemistry? If he should choose to concentrate in one of the natural sciences ought he nevertheless pursue a minor—in sociology, for example—to prepare himself specifically for the advanced work in the related subjects in the grad-

2 See James H. Tufts, *Education and Training for Social Work* (New York: Russell Sage Foundation. 1923). pp. 131–141: American Association of Social Work, *Education for the Public Social Services* (Chapel Hill, North Carolina: The University of North Carolina Press, 1942), pp. 47–52: and Irving Weissman and Mary R. Baker, *Education for Social Workers in the Public Social Services* (New York: Council on Social Work Education, 1959), vol. 7, pp. 135–136.

3 Werner W. Boehm, *Objectives of the Social Work Curriculum of the Future* (New York: Council on Social Work Education, 1959), vol. 1, p. 171.

uate school? And, lastly, what ought the future social worker know outside his professional field and the related disciplines to assume the broader
responsibilities of public and private life as a citizen, a homemaker, and
an effective human being generally? Definitive answers cannot be given
to most of these questions because of the difficulty of executing carefully controlled researches into the complex of forces at work in the individual's own particular life and in his education. Hence, most professional groups have laid down certain policies on the basis of informed
judgments as to the qualities required in a professional worker and the
types of educational experiences likely to produce, or at least influence,
these qualities.

Looking at the field of medicine again one can observe over the years
a change in point of view with regard to premedical requirements in the
various disciplines. After the publication of the Flexner report in 1910,
which called attention to the inadequacy of instruction in the basic and
medical sciences, the medical schools laid considerable stress on requirements in biology, chemistry, and physics. Little attention was then given
to the humanistic and social science fields. Later, however, the dominant
school of thought imposed a longer period of premedical education (now
normally four years) and urged students to pursue a broad program of
liberal studies in preparation for the study and practice of medicine. To
a large extent this shift in policy resulted from consideration of questions
related to the nature of medical practice and the requirements of life
generally in today's complex world. But the change also rested on a few
research studies of the relationship between the kinds and amounts of
education pursued in the undergraduate years and success in the medical
school.[4] These studies showed that beyond a minimum requirement in
the sciences the student could elect any combination of courses, or
major in any department, without handicapping himself in the study of
medicine.

Although generally acknowledging a preference for the social sciences, educators in social work, with few exceptions, have also taken the
position that a broad education in a variety of fields according to the students' interests would better serve their later needs than a heavy concentration in one, even one of the social sciences.[5] On this point, two of the
leading students of social work education have expressed the views that
a broad major in the arts and sciences is basic to graduate professional

[4] See study by Earl J. McGrath, "What Subjects Should the Premedical Student
Study?," *Journal of the Association of American Medical Colleges*, 20:273–280,
September 1945.
[5] Ernest V. Hollis and Alice L. Taylor, *Social Work Education in the United
States* (New York: Columbia University Press, 1951).

study in social work,[6] and that "The undergraduate concentration should not include concepts and experiences that require the intellectual and social maturation associated with later stages of graduate professional development."[7] Hence, it was considered desirable in this study of education for social work to investigate the relationships between the curricular patterns of the undergraduate years and the students' records in schools of social work. Specifically, insofar as possible it was decided that the policy of emphasizing a broad liberal education as preparation for advanced study in social work should be evaluated.[8] In the concrete, answers were sought to such questions as these: On the average do students who major in the social sciences make better grades in a school of social work than those who concentrate in one of the other major divisions of knowledge? Do students who achieve high grades in their undergraduate careers, regardless of their special intellectual interests, also maintain superior records in their later professional education?

To get answers to these questions in as objective form as possible an inquiry was designed which would relate the undergraduate academic records of 200 social work students to their records in their professional studies. All of these 200 persons had completed the requirements for a master's degree in a school of social work during the year 1961. Through the deans of schools of social work transcripts were obtained for each student covering all courses taken and all grades received in both undergraduate and professional courses. Some of the original cases had to be eliminated because no specific grades had been assigned in the graduate years or because of other inadequacies in the records. Insofar as can be determined the remaining cases do not constitute an atypical selection either of the schools of social work, of the colleges, or of the students. It can be assumed, therefore, that insofar as the findings are valid for these institutions and students they would be representative of all others who completed the master's degree in social work during 1961.

The first analysis of the transcripts dealt with the amount of instruction these 200 graduates of schools of social work had received in each of the major divisions of knowledge in their undergraduate education. Table 11 shows the total number of hours of credit received by these students in six undergraduate fields: (1) the humanities, (2) the natural sciences, (3) the social sciences, with a separate figure for sociology, (4) social

[6] *Ibid.*, p. 156.
[7] *Ibid.*, p. 182.
[8] For a prior, more comprehensive study of the total social work curriculum, see *The Social Work Curriculum Study* of the Council on Social Work Education (1959), published in thirteen volumes.

TABLE 11.  AMOUNT OF INSTRUCTION IN VARIOUS DIVISIONS OF KNOWLEDGE
RECEIVED BY 200 SOCIAL WORK STUDENTS IN THEIR UNDERGRADUATE YEARS

|  | Total semester hours | Percentage | Average credit hours |
|---|---|---|---|
| Humanities | 9,953.32 | 38.62 | 49.57 |
| Science | 3,091.68 | 12.00 | 15.46 |
| Social science/Sociology | 6,586.34/2,937.33 | 25.56/11.40 | 32.93/14.69 |
| Social welfare | 571.32 | 2.22 | 2.86 |
| Applied courses, other vocations | 1,771.65 | 6.87 | 8.86 |
| Miscellaneous | 859.35 | 3.33 | 4.30 |
| TOTAL | 25,770.99 | 100.00 | 128.85 |

welfare, (5) other vocational fields such as business administration, nursing, and theology, and (6) miscellaneous, which includes military science and physical education. This table also shows the percentage of instruction in each of the categories and the average number of credit hours of course work students pursued in each field.

Several significant facts stand out in this table relating to the combination of instructional units in the several divisions of knowledge which constitute preparation for graduate social work studies. First, on the average these students received a considerable amount of instruction in the humanities and relatively little in the natural sciences. Almost two-fifths of their work was in the fields of literature, foreign languages, philosophy, and art, while the average in biology, chemistry, physics, mathematics, and the other sciences was only 12 per cent. It is interesting that the total of 38.62 per cent in the humanities even exceeds the aggregate instruction in the whole range of social science subjects which amounted to 36.96 per cent.[9]

The social science figures were broken down into two subgroups, one of which included all the constituent fields except sociology. Here the figures are 11.40 per cent for sociology and 25.56 per cent for all the other subjects in the social science division. The small percentage, 2.22, in the social welfare subjects seems surprising because 140 colleges recognized by the Council on Social Work Education offer such instruction and 500 more offer at least one course in social welfare. The explanation may lie in the fact that when these students took their undergraduate work there were far fewer courses in social welfare available at the undergrad-

[9] For early recommendations to correct lack of emphasis on science and social science courses, see "Prerequisites for Admission to Schools of Social Work: A Report of the Curriculum Committee of the American Association of Schools of Social Work," in *Social Service Review,* September 1937, p. 471, and Esther L. Brown, *Social Work as a Profession* (New York: Russell Sage Foundation, 1942), pp. 56–57.

TABLE 12.  NUMBER OF YEARS BETWEEN OBTAINING UNDERGRADUATE DEGREE
AND ADMISSION TO GRADUATE SCHOOL OF SOCIAL WORK
*Average amount of graduate work per student: 60.05 credits (semester hours)*

|  | Cases | Percentage |
|---|---|---|
| Students who waited two years or less before entering graduate school | 111 | 55.5 |
| Students who waited from two to ten years before entering graduate school | 57 | 28.5 |
| Students who waited more than ten years before entering graduate school | 32 | 16.0 |
|  | 200 | 100.0 |

uate level. Even now the profession generally does not favor making professional social welfare courses a part of the undergraduate curriculum.[10] The relatively large percentage of courses in other vocations suggests that schools of social work attract students who may have changed their vocational objectives at the end of their undergraduate careers or even much later in their lives. This latter inference is borne out by the figures in Table 12 which show that 44.5 per cent of these 200 graduates in social work did not enter the professional school until more than two years after receiving their bachelor's degrees. It should be observed, of course, that many of the latter were, nevertheless, employed in social work of one sort or another during the intervening years.

These figures as a whole show that graduate students in social work receive a fairly broad undergraduate education in the various major disciplines and that as a group they do not concentrate excessively in the social science fields. Even combining the percentages in social science and sociology the total is only 36.96 or slightly more than one-third of the total undergraduate curriculum. The aggregate of only 14.69 per cent in sociology reveals that customarily these students take about five courses, each bearing three hours of credit in this field. This is not enough credit in sociology to satisfy the almost universal requirements for a major in that field, or in any other. The variation above and below the average in all fields, however, also shows that some students concentrate very heavily in the social sciences and the humanities, but rarely in the natural sciences. To the degree that this concentration is excessive the objective of a broad preparatory education in the liberal arts disciplines is reduced.

Two items of particular concern in this inquiry were (1) the rela-

[10] For a good evaluation of this preference and the problems of selection and timing in preprofessional education which result, see Charlotte Towle, *The Learner in Education for the Professions: As Seen in Education for Social Work* (Chicago: The University of Chicago Press, 1954), pp. 205–217.

TABLE 13

| Correlation Coefficient Between Graduate Grade and: | *Coefficient* |
|---|---|
| Number of years between graduate and undergraduate work | + .046 |
| Humanities undergraduate credit | + .046 |
| Humanities undergraduate grade | + .342 |
| Science undergraduate credit | + .012 |
| Science undergraduate grade | + .355 |
| Social science undergraduate credit | + .016 |
| Social science undergraduate grade | + .344 |
| Sociology undergraduate credit | + .064 |
| Sociology undergraduate grade | + .072 |
| Combined social science and sociology undergraduate credit | + .052 |
| Combined social science and sociology undergraduate grade | + .376 |
| Social welfare undergraduate credit | + .058 |
| Social welfare undergraduate grade | + .186 |
| Total undergraduate credit | + .163 |
| Total undergraduate grade | + .374 |

tionship between the number of hours taken in one of the three major divisions of knowledge and the student's record in the graduate school of social work, and (2) the relationship between the grades received at both levels of instruction. Table 13 reveals these relationships.

The most obvious fact disclosed by these figures is the rather low correlations between all the factors studied. To the question, what undergraduate subjects best prepare students to complete a program in the school of social work successfully, these figures in Table 13 supply the answer that the amount of instruction in the various major branches of knowledge is not significant. The correlations vary from +.012 in science to +.064 in sociology, neither of which is significant. Several qualifications should be made to this generalization about the value of various programs of undergraduate education and success in social work courses at the graduate level.

In the first place, none of the students who failed or who dropped out of a social work program is included in these figures. It could be argued that those who discontinued for one reason or another had either pursued more or less instruction in one of the branches of knowledge than the average student and were thus adversely affected by an unbalanced preparation. This study can neither affirm nor deny this proposition. Only a comparison study of the dropouts would shed light on this matter.

A second factor which may reduce these correlations is the narrow spread of grades in professional courses. Almost all students in these graduate courses who completed the requirements for a degree received grades of A or B; only rarely were C's or D's given. Hence, the correlations would probably have been different if a greater range of achievement, or at least finer gradations of achievement, had been established at the graduate level. The insignificant relationships shown in Table 13 do, however, suggest that concentration in a particular field such as physics, sociology, or English places the future student of social work under no handicap. Moreover, these figures tend to sustain the profession in its position that a broad and varied preparation in liberal arts subjects provides a suitable basis for future professional study.

Table 13 also reveals the relationships between the grade point average in undergraduate courses classified by the major divisions of knowledge and the grade point average in professional courses in social work at the graduate level. Here again the correlations are low, ranging from +.342 between undergraduate grades in the humanities to +.376 between the social sciences and graduate grades in all subjects.

A very significant fact appears in the low correlation between undergraduate grades in sociology and graduate grades (+.072). Since the correlation between the combined grades in undergraduate social science (including sociology) and the graduate grades is +.376 it appears that social science courses other than sociology completed with high grades are better predictors of high grades in graduate schools of social work than high grades in undergraduate courses in sociology. It may be that this latter low correlation results from the practice of graduate instructors repeating much of the basic instruction in sociology given in the undergraduate years. If this is the case the advantage of the highly successful undergraduate would to a degree be canceled out in his graduate courses. In any event, these correlations in the social science fields deserve further detailed analysis in relationship to the content of instruction at both levels. The general conclusion drawn from correlations of undergraduate grades and graduate grades in schools of social work is that the former are better predictors of success in graduate work than the amount of instruction taken in one of the major divisions of knowledge. Good students tend to be good students at both levels though the correlations are not very high.

Table 14 sheds additional light on these relationships. In each subdivision of knowledge the students with relatively large amounts of instruction were treated separately, and correlations run between their undergraduate grades and their grades in schools of social work. Here the results are at variance with the same correlations for the whole group of students in each of these subdivisions. Apparently, for students who concentrate heavily in the humanities (over seventy credits) the relation-

TABLE 14. CORRELATIONS BETWEEN UNDERGRADUATE GRADES IN VARIOUS
SUBJECT FIELDS AND GRADUATE GRADES

|  | Coefficient |
|---|---|
| OVER 70 CREDITS IN HUMANITIES (9 CASES): | |
| Correlation of humanities undergraduate grade with graduate grade | + .045 |
| Correlation of total undergraduate grade with graduate grade | + .077 |
| OVER 24 CREDITS IN SCIENCE (18 CASES): | |
| Correlation of science undergraduate grade with graduate grade | + .416 |
| Correlation of total undergraduate grade with graduate grade | + .371 |
| OVER 42 CREDITS IN SOCIAL SCIENCE (27 CASES): | |
| Correlation of social science undergraduate grade with graduate grade | + .487 |
| Correlation of total undergraduate grade with graduate grade | + .387 |
| OVER 24 CREDITS IN SOCIOLOGY (24 CASES): | |
| Correlation of sociology undergraduate grade with graduate grade | + .392 |
| Correlation of total undergraduate grade with graduate grade | + .476 |
| OVER 66 CREDITS IN COMBINED SOCIAL SCIENCE AND SOCIOLOGY (15 CASES): | |
| Correlation of combined social science and sociology undergraduate graduate with graduate grade | + .310 |
| Correlation of total undergraduate grade with graduate grade | + .350 |
| OVER 15 CREDITS IN SOCIAL WELFARE (4 CASES): | |
| Correlation of social welfare undergraduate grade with graduate grade | + .876 |
| Correlation of total undergraduate grade with graduate grade | + .936 |

ships between grades at both levels are less congruous than those of their fellow majors who concentrate less intensively in this field. The correlation is only +.045, not significant. On the other hand, in other categories studied—for example, social science, sociology, and the combination of the two—the correlations between the grades of those who took relatively large amounts of undergraduate instruction in these fields and grades in graduate courses in social work are relatively high, as high as +.487 between undergraduate social science and graduate work. To a degree this high correlation may be explained by the fact that some undergraduate social welfare courses carry sociology titles and numbers and would, therefore, be classified under the later category.

The most striking correlation is that between undergraduate social welfare courses in excess of fifteen credits and graduate grades, +.876. Unfortunately, there were only four such cases and consequently no valid generalization can be drawn, but it is clear that these students for some reason ran truer to form in the graduate years than any other group. The correlation of total undergraduate grades for these four students with graduate grades (+.936, almost perfect) suggests that they were a very stable, highly selected group with strong motivation toward social work, but a further study ought to be made of a larger group of students. If the same correlations were discovered the inference could be drawn that schools of social work would get their best students from among those who in their undergraduate years had pursued more than fifteen hours of instruction in social welfare courses. This finding raises serious questions about admissions policies as well as about the position of the profession toward undergraduate courses in social welfare. A more exhaustive and detailed study of this matter is urgently needed to clarify the validity of established policies.

These findings with respect to the amount of instruction taken in the undergraduate years and grades in a professional school of social work are confirmed by another related study completed earlier by Fletcher and Osborne.[11] These investigators reported that "The number of social science courses taken as an undergraduate seems to have little bearing upon graduate performance." They also state that in fact as far as the proportion of undergraduate social science courses taken is concerned, the "influence is negative, upon the graduate performance." In another respect their findings parallel those in this study, for they report that "The students making the best grades in college tend to give the best performance in the Institute of Social Work." Fletcher and Osborn's results are especially significant because the undergraduates they studied all came from accredited Michigan colleges and they all pursued their graduate social work courses in one institution, the Institute of Social Work.

The figures in neither study unfortunately give any indication of the success of these students when they assumed their responsibilities as practitioners of social work. It has been argued that a broad undergraduate preparation cultivates qualities of personality and faculties of mind which are highly valuable in the daily practice of social work, but which may not be measured by grades in graduate social work courses. Liberal education would thus be justified on other grounds than preparation for professional study, but if so, efforts should be made to identify these qualities of mind and personality and to measure their presence or absence among graduate students after they have completed their training and entered the profession.

SUMMARY, CONCLUSIONS, AND UNANSWERED QUESTIONS

The analysis of undergraduate preparation of these 200 persons who eventually acquired master's degrees in a professional school of social

[11] Ralph C. Fletcher and T. Curtis Osborn, "Undergraduate Preparation for Graduate Work," *Compass*, 28:12–16, September 1947.

work shows that there is little positive correlation between the number of undergraduate courses taken in the social sciences in general, or sociology in particular, and grades in graduate schools of social work. Since all the students involved had some instruction in the social sciences the question whether a person with a bachelor's degree without any sociology, economics, political science, or any related subject, could succeed at the graduate level is left unanswered. The correlations between grades in undergraduate courses classified as natural sciences, social sciences, and humanities, and success in graduate courses in social work suggest, however, that a student with no social science preparation could perform satisfactorily at the graduate level if he had been a high-grade student at the undergraduate level.

In fact, insofar as grades can be assumed to be a measure of success, a good undergraduate record in any field of study is at present the best guarantee of success in a graduate program in social work. The correlations between grades in the major divisions of knowledge in the undergraduate years are not especially high, but they are positive in all fields. Schools of social work which give particular attention to the average grade record in the undergraduate years will more likely admit students who can successfully complete a graduate course of study than those who give primary attention to the course elections of applicants. A student who majored in physics or literature with a good record is doubtless a better risk than one who majored in sociology with a mediocre record.

Nevertheless, those who advocate a broad liberal education as preparation for the study of social work at the graduate level seem to be on sound ground insofar as the findings in this study are concerned if consideration is also given to the quality of the undergraduate record. At least it can be said that those who bring such a broad preparation to their graduate studies achieve as satisfactory records as those who concentrate heavily in any of the undergraduate major divisions of knowledge. And it can be assumed that there are other nonprofessional values in a ranging undergraduate education not reflected in the correlations in this study. There are also educational values related to private and public life completed outside the practice of a profession which should be enhanced by broad learning. Until more comprehensive and more searching research has been completed, the prevailing policy of encouraging free election of courses in the undergraduate years seems justified by successful performance in professional programs of social work.

Many questions, however, remain to be answered. For example, how much instruction in sociology and the other social sciences can be considered a defensible bare minimum for advanced study in social work?

Concretely, will one basic course in sociology, economics, political science, psychology, and anthropology suffice, or should one of these fields be penetrated in depth, that is, would a student with twenty-four hours in sociology, and study in the higher branches of the subject which that implies, be better prepared to succeed in a school of social work than one who had spread his options in social science over three or four fields? Or are both depth and spread essential? At present the limited knowledge produced by available controlled research does not supply definitive answers to these questions.

Moreover, the very large and most significant question, concerning the relation between the amount of various kinds of instruction and the grades obtained in both undergraduate and graduate fields, and success as a practitioner of social work, remains unanswered. It is hypothetically possible that no positive relationship exists among any of these factors. A recent study of grades attained in medical schools by graduates of McGill University and success as a physician reveals no significant relationships.[12] Obviously these results do not mean that the formal study of medicine is not essential, but the effective practice apparently involves human factors and qualities not reflected in grades in medical school courses. Hence, those who achieve high grades in a medical school seem to be no more successful on the average in the practice of their profession than those whose academic records are less distinguished. The same results would doubtless be derived from a study of practitioners of social work. Studies ought to be made with particular respect to the kinds of undergraduate and graduate instruction the practitioner has had, and his later success in understanding the milieu in which the professional worker necessarily carries on his duties, and his capacity to deal with human problems in a perceptive and effective manner.

In the absence of such objective analysis it would seem desirable to permit the undergraduate to major in any discipline to which he is drawn by his own intellectual interests and abilities. It would seem desirable to advise him to gain a basic knowledge of the social science fields, including economics and political science which are now neglected by many students who concentrate in sociology. Moreover, until contradictory evidence is produced the prospective student of social work, in the interests of more effective practice and a richer personal life, ought to be encouraged to study as widely as possible in the natural sciences and the humanities. This type of broad preparation, which not only lays the

[12] R. C. A. Hunter, J. G. Sohrenge, and A. E. Schwartzman, "A Fifteen Year Follow-Up Study of Medical Graduates," *The Canadian Medical Association Journal,* vol. 87 (October 20, 1962,) pp. 865–868.

groundwork for study in a professional field but also provides the maturing adult with the opportunity for the broad education essential to understanding the world in which he is to live, would seem to be justified by the present findings of research, inadequate though they may be, as well as by the opinions of those who see the work of a professional practitioner in the larger complex of life.

## Chapter 5

# INTERVIEWS WITH PERSONNEL IN SCHOOLS OF SOCIAL WORK

IN ORDER TO SUPPLEMENT AND FOCUS THE ANALYSES OF RELEVANT literature, inventories, transcripts, and school catalogs, visits were made to nine of the fifty-six accredited schools of social work in the United States. These schools were selected to give a reasonable range according to such criteria as geographical location, size, age, and auspices. While the primary concern was with persons responsible for the graduate social work program in each institution, it was also possible to give some consideration to the place of undergraduate education for social welfare since five of the nine institutions offer a core of undergraduate social welfare courses recognized by the Council on Social Work Education and three others offer at least one undergraduate social welfare course. Two or three days were spent at each school interviewing university and school administrative officers, faculty members, and students.

### ATTITUDES OF UNIVERSITY ADMINISTRATORS

In each university an administrator with either a direct or dotted-line administrative relationship to the school was interviewed. Usually this was the president or his representative.

Without exception these persons declared themselves to be strongly committed to the importance of a broad and balanced liberal education at the undergraduate level. Most of these administrators stated that there was no question about the necessity for such undergraduate preparation for any graduate study, and several believed that it was the undergraduate preparation of choice also for immediate employment in any field. Several of their comments follow:

A firm liberal arts preparation is the only acceptable undergraduate foundation for any professional study.

There should be no professional education at the undergraduate level. Liberal education is the best preparation for any profession.

A broad and liberal education is the best preparation for any graduate study, or for any employment.

A broad liberal arts preparation is best for any graduate education, including social work.

Professional education should only be graduate education.

If we have sound general liberal education we can then move with greater assurance into specific graduate work. Perhaps even more than some other fields, social work graduate education requires broad and liberal undergraduate preparation rather than a specific major.

## ATTITUDES OF SCHOOL ADMINISTRATORS

Despite the fact that approximately one-half of the schools visited offer undergraduate social welfare concentrations and most of the others offer at least one undergraduate social welfare course, the school deans and directors tended to feel that at least so far as preparation for graduate social work education is concerned a liberal undergraduate education is best. Most of their comments underlined that of one dean who said, "A broad and liberal education is best. There is simply no substitute for it."

While several of the school administrators rejected outright any possibility of an undergraduate program of worth being other than "broad and liberal," three discussed the possible justification of an undergraduate social welfare major because it already was—or could be—developed within a liberal arts framework. One dean stated that the undergraduate social welfare sequence at that institution had been revised fairly recently "to weed out vocational aspects. Within university policy it had to be justified as liberal education. Now it emerges as a solid liberal arts major."

While the majority, then, rejected undergraduate social welfare education as appropriate preparation for graduate social work education, a few were ready to consider its potential for development *as* liberal education. Only one felt that it was a relatively sound way of preparing persons for immediate employment even if it were practicable to ensure that the employment was at, for example, a case aide level.

## GENERAL FACULTY ATTITUDES

Of the more than sixty faculty persons interviewed at these schools, almost all considered that any undergraduate preparation other than liberal arts was less than optimum preparation. Several believed that the growing developments in undergraduate social welfare education, marked by the publication of *Social Welfare Content in Undergraduate Education,*[1] made it necessary to take a new look at the practicability of developing such programs within a liberal arts framework.

Nonetheless, the overwhelming consensus was that any undergraduate preparation other than liberal arts prepares the student less well for either graduate study or employment in social work.

### FACULTY DISSATISFACTIONS CONCERNING UNDERGRADUATE PREPARATION

The most frequently encountered dissatisfactions were variations on the theme, *Why Can't Johnny Read* (or *Write,* or *Spell,* or *Punctuate*)? A few faculty members felt that the general criticism concerning students' inability to communicate effectively in either oral or written fashion was not true. Most faculty persons ranged themselves along a continuum from an observation that "most students are not well grounded in communication skills" to the statement that "too many students are relatively illiterate."

No other dissatisfaction was mentioned so often. Several persons suggested that it was a reflection not simply of inadequate undergraduate preparation in, for example, English composition, but of general weakness in this area from elementary school forward. Nor did they ascribe these shortcomings primarily to teachers of English. Their feeling was that all educators share the responsibility for the situation by, among other things, their willingness to accept inadequately written themes and assignments. One instructor summarized the viewpoint of many:

> Our students' great and perplexing deficiency is incapacity to do expository writing. They cannot organize and, hence, cannot conceptualize. This is a fundamental weakness in the whole educational system. This is especially important for social work because of the importance of the ability to communicate.

The next most often mentioned deficiency concerned the humanities. Many faculty persons felt that the lack of such subjects as philosophy, logic, and history in the backgrounds of many students was weakening:

[1] Council on Social Work Education, New York, 1962.

Too many students are weak in the humanities and, hence, exhibit a lack of sustained logical thinking.

The primary need of undergraduate preparation is to help the student to learn to think, to integrate, and to relate. The humanities play a crucial role in facilitating these.

Several instructors indicated that what they were criticizing might sometimes be the teaching rather than the content. History was cited as an example: A student might have been exposed to courses in history and still not have been helped to appreciate the sweep and implication of historical development. It was noted that a concern for dates and battles scarcely prepared a student to look at the past in order to have more effective appreciation of the present and the future.

Other areas of deficiency mentioned fairly often were natural science, mathematics, and foreign languages. These were not felt to be such pressing deficiencies as the above mentioned.

FACULTY SATISFACTIONS CONCERNING
UNDERGRADUATE PREPARATION

Most faculty members favored the social sciences—especially sociology and psychology, in that order—as appropriate undergraduate majors for persons planning to undertake a graduate social work program. However, there was some feeling that there has been a tendency, both within professions and within universities, to "go overboard" for the social sciences as appropriate preparation for any human relations field. These faculty members were not discounting the usefulness of the social sciences but were mainly concerned with the possibility that such a major can still result in relatively narrow preparation and can "drain off" time and effort, some of which could be profitably directed toward the humanities.

Most agreed that today's students tend to have had more undergraduate sociology and psychology than students in earlier years and that, for the most part, this is good. However, several lamented the fact that for many students preparation in the social sciences tended to be a series of introductory or survey-type courses rather than an exploration in depth of one or more of these social sciences. They spoke of an "ideal" social science major as one that developed on a firm foundation of the humanities and the natural sciences. They also mentioned that such preparation was rarely encountered.

There was also some feeling that a number of their best students had not had a specific or single major, but rather had had what they referred to as "genuine liberal arts preparation" which seemed to be a restatement of the "ideal" undergraduate curriculum mentioned above.

Strengths in current graduate students mentioned by many faculty persons were their real interest in and concern for people, and their intense desire to help. However, along with this often went a demand for quick answers and a consequent frustration at the lack—and the possible inappropriateness—of these in social work.

Many faculty persons felt that the particular undergraduate college attended was more important than the major completed. "A 'C' average from X College usually reflects a better student than a 'B' average from Y College." Some persons seemed bemused by the halo effect of certain prestigious colleges, but several described clearly what they were thinking about. Most of them identified the college climate—stimulus, kind of standards, expectations, etc.—as being the factor of crucial importance.

ATTITUDES OF STUDENTS

A small group of graduate students was interviewed at each school. They seemed able to look both critically and appreciatively at the undergraduate preparation they had had and many of their comments, particularly those concerning areas of felt deficiency, were remarkably similar to those of faculty members.

Almost without exception the students felt that they had not had sufficient preparation in English (particularly in communication skills) and philosophy.

Most felt strongly that a broad and balanced liberal arts preparation was the best preparation. One student remarked, "This is especially important because graduate social work education is specific. Its value is increased if the specificity rests on a broad liberal arts base."

Most students had had either a social science major (most often sociology) or had had a concentration of social science courses along with their major. Several of the sociology graduates believed that their undergraduate major had made some of their graduate work repetitious. On the other hand, some other sociology graduates thought that it had simply made their graduate work more meaningful.

Whatever the major, there was general recognition that they had learned most from instructors whose teaching was conceptual rather than information giving. They pointed out, too, "You often take a teacher, not a course."

With a few exceptions, most believed that undergraduate preparation in social welfare was not the best preparation for graduate social work education. The great majority, however, felt that every student should have at least one introductory or survey-type course in social welfare which would be a legitimate part of a liberal arts program because of the growing institutionalization of social welfare.

While some thought that undergraduate social welfare education would also be inadequate preparation (as compared with a "broader" liberal arts preparation) even for limited employment responsibilities, most believed that realistically there had to be some "break-through" in the present social work personnel situation. Since the graduate schools were not likely in the foreseeable future to be able to meet the need, it would become increasingly necessary for persons to be prepared at the undergraduate level for immediate social welfare employment. Most students—like most faculty members—felt that this would only be appropriate if the social work profession were able adequately to define job responsibilities and the required preparation to discharge those responsibilities effectively, and to hold to these.

Many students recalled having resisted enrollment in undergraduate statistics and research courses and of these many believed that, faced with the situation again, they would continue to resist. Several believed that rather than requiring persons to take such courses, the same objectives might be realized more effectively if the regular courses in, for example, the social sciences were more research oriented. "Courses with this kind of orientation, whether in social science, humanities or natural science, help people to communicate, to order data, and to systematize."

Few students were opinionated with respect to a particular major being the "best" major. While most came from the social sciences, and most of these would again choose the social sciences, many reflected a view verbalized by one student, "There is no one best major so long as the preparation has been broad and liberal."

### Student Participation in Curriculum Development

Most schools had an active student organization and most of these took a formal or informal interest in curriculum development, forwarding suggestions to the faculty for consideration. In addition to a student organization, several schools had a student-faculty committee which acted as a bridge between students and faculty with respect to curriculum and other matters.

It seemed clear that in most instances students had taken a serious interest in curriculum development and had often made thoughtful suggestions which received consideration and, in several instances, had resulted in specific change. In one school, for example, student suggestions played a direct role in the reorganizing of a sequence of courses.

No student organization was reported to have discussed or taken a point of view with respect to undergraduate preparation for graduate social work education.

### PARTICIPATION IN CURRICULUM DEVELOPMENT BY ALUMNI AND OTHERS

Each school had an alumni association, most of which seemed to be active and with some interest in curriculum development. Several alumni associations had been involved in such activities as follow-up surveys and workshops designed to draw reactions to and suggestions about the curriculum. One alumni organization was particularly active in this area with frequent feedback concerning curriculum, research studies, and the like.

The schools were in continuing touch with agency personnel, many of whom were also field instructors, and drew on these persons for reaction and consultation concerning curriculum.

A few schools had an advisory committee comprising social work and non-social work persons, and believed that these were useful. They noted that it was important to spend enough time to use such a committee effectively, otherwise it tended to be window dressing and rather superficial "involvement" of lay and professional persons in the conduct of the school.

The schools believed that the great majority of members of their alumni and other school-related groups consider that professional social work education should only be at the graduate level, and that the best undergraduate preparation is a broad liberal arts program. This impression is supported by the analysis of the inventories submitted by social work practitioners.

### CURRENT CURRICULUM ISSUES FACING THE SCHOOLS

There was no single issue that was readily identified by all the schools as being particularly pressing other than the day-to-day endeavors to build increasingly effective programs, obtain additional faculty and higher budgets, etc.

While all schools gave attention to a continuing review of curriculum, four of the schools indicated that their present primary objective in this was to try to "open up" the professional curriculum so as to permit electives or more electives. They believed this to be an area of concern both to faculty and to students, the latter having moved through an undergraduate preparation which permitted at least some flexibility to a graduate curriculum which, because of required courses, was almost wholly rigid.

Those schools which had either an undergraduate social welfare major or one or more undergraduate social welfare courses were concerned with developing these programs away from a vocational or quasi-vocational and toward a liberal arts orientation.

## LIBERAL EDUCATION ADMISSIONS REQUIREMENTS

The catalogs of most of these schools (and of most of the other accredited schools) make explicit reference to the desirability of a liberal undergraduate education as preparation for graduate social work education. Many also indicate a preference for a concentration of courses in the social sciences. The following are statements from catalogs of the schools visited:

> [The school prefers students to have had a] well-integrated liberal arts course including such subjects as philosophy, psychology, ethics, economics, history, anthropology, sociology, political science, government, and statistics.

> Undergraduate and/or graduate curriculum in liberal arts with studies in the behavioral and social sciences preferred.

> [Admission] normally is limited to graduates of accredited colleges or universities who have completed a well-rounded program of general education. Such a program includes study in the humanities, social sciences, and biological sciences, all of which are important preparation for study in a graduate school of social work.

> Completion of 30 [semester] hours of academic work well distributed in the social and biological sciences and in the humanities.

> It is expected that the student will enter graduate training with a well-rounded liberal education, including a basic knowledge of the behavioral sciences.

Many of the catalogs from the schools not visited refer specifically to the importance of "preparation in liberal arts" and the appropriateness of a major in one of the social sciences.

Along with the above, most of the schools require at least a "B minus" average in undergraduate work unless there are circumstances that warrant special consideration. Many also require marginal applicants to take the Graduate Record Examination or a comparable test, and sometimes to make up undergraduate deficiencies without credit before or immediately after admission.

Beyond the objective grade point average the schools indicated their interest in the span of subject matter, the progression in performance, and, in some instances, the particular college attended.

## INVOLVEMENT OF OTHER DEPARTMENTS WITH THE SCHOOL OF SOCIAL WORK

In general, members of the faculties of the liberal arts departments had little relationship with the schools of social work. Very seldom has an entire course been offered within the school by a member of another department, although occasionally such persons (usually from the sociology or the psychology department) may participate in a particular social work course or be brought in to give one or two lectures.

Relationships between the schools visited and the liberal arts departments in their universities seemed generally to be cordial and cooperative, and occasionally members of other departments (again usually sociology and psychology) may be involved in joint research projects and on student research committees.

In one school, representatives from other departments were included on the curriculum committee and appeared to have some influence on curriculum development. The curriculum committees in the other schools did not include representatives from other departments, and even at an informal level other departments did not seem to exert influence in curriculum matters.

Generally the social work graduate curriculum seemed to be almost wholly developed within the schools without real influence from the liberal arts or other non-social work faculties, and within the university subject usually to the scrutiny of an all-university or senate committee. Such scrutiny might have direct effect in terms of initiating a new course or a new degree program, but seemed rarely to have any effect with respect to course content or focus.

Another reflection of the limited academic interrelationships between the schools and departments may be the fact that very few students have taken any course work outside the school of social work. Even in schools where electives were available, these were usually social work electives rather than courses available in other departments.

There are objective factors which contribute to this situation. For some schools the matter of geography may be a primary factor: Several schools of social work are distant from the main university campus. In many universities the schedule pattern does not readily permit taking courses outside the school: For example, students who are in field placement Wednesday, Thursday, and Friday may not be able to take courses in other departments scheduled on the usual university pattern of classes being held on Tuesdays and Thursdays, or Mondays, Wednesdays, and Fridays. Despite such realistic factors there might be situations in which arrangements for taking courses in other departments could be worked out.

A corollary situation is also found in many schools. Relatively few students from other departments take courses within the school of social work. Several faculty members indicated that while this is inevitable and often desirable in any kind of professional school, there were certain courses within the social work curriculum which might benefit students from other departments and in which the inclusion of students from other departments might also benefit the social work students.

In the institutions in which undergraduate social welfare courses were offered, instructors from the school of social work tended to be involved in other departments, usually sociology since that department was the one in which undergraduate social welfare courses were found if they were not offered within the school of social work.

All the schools visited offered counseling to undergraduate students in other departments who were considering social work either as a possible area for graduate study or for employment. Again most students were referred from departments of sociology but also came from other departments, particularly psychology and education. The faculty of the school of social work tended to encourage such students (especially those considering graduate social work education) to take a broad and balanced liberal undergraduate education.

## The School "Climate"

None of the schools visited reflected an approach preoccupied with how-to-do-it techniques, but rather a concern for the teaching of principles and concepts.

Along with appropriate concern with methods instruction there seemed to be overarching consideration of social issues and policies within a research-oriented frame of reference. This is not to say that the school faculties were doing this to their satisfaction, but each articulated awareness of the significance of conceptually based instruction and of the need to implement this across the curriculum. The schools seemed to be giving a good deal of attention to the importance of identification of educational objectives within the curriculum generally, and within the sequences and courses in the curriculum. The impact of the Curriculum Study[2] was evident in some of these developments. The 1962 Curriculum Policy Statement was also mentioned by several as a framework within which curriculum developments could be facilitated. These factors seemed to contribute to what one faculty person described as "a feeling of academic excitement—things are on the move."

For such reasons, it may be becoming less appropriate to consider liberal education and professional education in dichotomous terms. Many instructors were convinced that graduate social work courses, while professionally oriented and offered "for use," could still be taught in liberal fashion. "It is a poor professional course that is taught in vocational fashion. Any course can be taught within a liberal framework."

VIEWS ON UNDERGRADUATE SOCIAL WELFARE COURSES

In each school there was consensus, and in several schools unanimity, with respect to the following: There is no place at the undergraduate level for a major concentration of social welfare courses and (especially) there should be no kind of field experience. This viewpoint was also voiced by most faculty persons who were interviewed at schools which had an undergraduate social welfare major.

With two of the schools there was a proviso to the above attitude: There would have been consensus that there was a place at the undergraduate level for a major concentration of social work courses if the profession were able to classify social work positions and responsibilities, and make such classifications "stick."

Most of the faculty persons who believed that there was not only a place but a need for undergraduate social welfare curriculums stated that the major justification was that of personnel need in the field, and that increasing numbers of students would have to be prepared for employment following completion of the bachelor's degree. For those persons planning to go on to graduate social work education they agreed with the overwhelming majority of all faculty persons interviewed: The best preparation for graduate social work education is a broad and balanced liberal education.

Several faculty members said that their views might be different if

2 Werner W. Boehm *et al., The Social Work Curriculum Study*, 14 volumes (New York: Council on Social Work Education, 1959).

existing undergraduate social welfare concentrations could be regeared so that they were distinctly liberal education rather than preprofessional education. "Preprofessional is just another word for vocational."

There was near unanimity that professional social work education should only be at the graduate level, and that the undergraduate-graduate continuum proposed in the Curriculum Study[3] was neither practicable nor appropriate. The following views were characteristic:

> Undergraduate social work education is best if thought of as liberal arts with a social work concern. It has some, but not much value as a recruiting device for graduate social work. However, it is not as good preparation for graduate social work as a broader liberal education.

> A full social work undergraduate major defeats the purpose of liberal education. Undergraduate social work education inevitably leads to too narrow a preparation.

> The only justification for undergraduate social work preparation is that it may motivate certain students to go on to graduate social work training, but they'd be better prepared to use the graduate education if they had had a broader and more liberal undergraduate preparation.

> Undergraduate social work courses get the students too narrow too soon. We can teach techniques when they get to graduate school, but they should bring a broad base of liberal education. There is too much specialization anyhow. They need diversity and generality.

> It would be appropriate to abolish the undergraduate social work major, as it negates the efforts to upgrade and professionalize. You turn out something you don't believe in. You tell the field "it's almost as good."

> Students from a liberal arts undergraduate major do better even in immediate public assistance employment than do graduates of undergraduate social work programs. The latter had preconceived ideas of self as worker that got in their way. They felt they knew more than they actually did.

Many faculty persons returned to an issue that troubled them and that was expressed by Bertram Beck when he described the failure of

[3] *Ibid,*

educators and practitioners to factor out those social work responsibilities which do and do not require professional preparation.[4]

Faculty members expressed their feelings about this as follows:

If the profession could establish adequate job classifications—and employ within those classifications—there would be a place for the undergraduate social welfare concentration.

I do not believe in an undergraduate social work major as a matter of preference, but of reality. It is probably necessary because of the market and might be all right if persons could be prepared for—and held to—limited responsibilities.

The profession and social work education have long dodged the responsibility of adequately classifying social work responsibilities. If this were done then one could consider both undergraduate and graduate social work education more realistically.

If there were real social work job classifications then undergraduate social work training might be developed, but only for specifically limited responsibilities.

Some faculty persons were mistrustful of the effects of job classifications in terms of appropriate professional responsibilities even if these could be worked out. "There is so much demand for people with any kind of preparation that levels of responsibility would become meaningless."

On the other hand, one faculty person stated that "if the worker can handle the responsibility let him move up to it, no matter what his preparation. After all, graduate education is only one way of preparing for social work."

Almost all faculty persons said that, because of the tremendous growth in social welfare and its institutionalization, it was appropriate to offer at least one undergraduate social welfare course (usually referred to as a "fields" course) as a part of the liberal education of any undergraduate. In addition to its function of informing, it was seen as a help to some students in developing or testing their interest in later social work studies. The following were indicative comments:

This kind of undergraduate course has validity today as a liberal arts course in its own right.

[4] Bertram M. Beck, "Job Definition: A First Step," in *Education for Social Work,* Proceedings of the Eleventh Annual Program Meeting of the Council on Social Work Education, 1963, pp. 29–32.

An occasional undergraduate social welfare course can be very useful, preferably offered in another department, such as sociology, so that there is less chance of it being identified as professional or preprofessional.

Two of the schools were developing undergraduate social welfare concentrations that seemed to approach what faculty members were speaking about when they discussed an "ideal" undergraduate social welfare major. In one school this program had been under way in its present form for several years and the faculty members closest to it expressed their conviction that "it *is* liberal education. It is theoretically and philosophically rather than practice oriented." In some universities the curriculum might have been identified as a social science divisional major rather than a social welfare major. It was concentrated essentially in the junior and senior years and comprised core courses in sociology and psychology, general courses (including specific requirements in statistics and logic), and a total of nine semester credits in social welfare courses. It included no field experience or observation. A faculty member observed:

> The graduate of this major has a social science core, an understanding of social welfare as an institution in our society, and an orderly and understanding way of thinking about his world. Such a student can use graduate social work education more constructively.

### Summary of Main Findings

1. The best undergraduate preparation for professional social work education is a broad and balanced liberal education.

2. Professional education for social work should remain at the graduate level. There should be no undergraduate-graduate continuum.

3. Within a liberal arts education the preferred majors are the social sciences, especially sociology.

4. Along with (3) there is a wish to include other social sciences (for example, economics and political science) rather than having a narrow preoccupation with, for example, sociology.

5. There is a general feeling that undergraduate background in the humanities tends to be slim, sometimes negligible. There is particular concern about students' inadequate preparation in English (specifically, inability to communicate, especially in written form) and lack of courses in philosophy (especially logic).

6. The natural sciences, too, tend to be slighted, with many students entering graduate school ignorant of even elementary concepts of biology.

7. Most of the graduate faculty members, university administrators, and graduate social work students interviewed are opposed to any substantial social work curriculum at the undergraduate level, and are specific about the inappropriateness of "methods" courses and field experience.

8. Many graduate faculty members acknowledge the usefulness and appropriateness of an undergraduate course or two which would consider social welfare as an important institution in our society. They see this as acceptable subject matter and justifiable as liberal education.

9. These graduate faculty members recognize the demands of the market, and the impossibility within the foreseeable future of meeting these demands through persons with full graduate education. Most do not feel that the best answer is to "settle for less." Rather, the professional schools should concentrate on preparing persons as effectively as possible at the graduate level; "pursuit of excellence." Such persons can "spark" the field, and at least gradually man the senior practitioner and supervisory positions.

10. Graduate faculty members acknowledge that most positions will continue to be filled by persons without graduate education and that this probably means the continuing growth of undergraduate social welfare programs. These should be oriented clearly within a liberal arts framework, and should be "academically respectable" in liberal arts terms.

11. Most faculty persons state that if the undergraduate student knows that he is going to go on to a graduate school of social work, he would be best advised not to take an undergraduate social welfare major. If, however, he is clearly going to go into social work employment at the end of his undergraduate preparation, then some of these faculty members accept the practicality, at least in terms of vocational utility, of undergraduate social welfare preparation.

12. Most faculty persons state that, even for immediate employment, an undergraduate social welfare major is not as effective preparation as is a more general and liberal program. They believe that it is more important to have developed a way of looking at man in society, with his problems and opportunities, than to have been exposed to specific social welfare courses.

13. There is a small but convinced group that feels that the above are not necessarily incompatible, namely, that it is practicable to offer an undergraduate social welfare major which also fulfills the expectations of a liberal arts program.

14. Practically no persons were encountered in any of the faculty, administrative, or student groups who favored the recommendation of

the Curriculum Study about the development of social work education on an undergraduate-graduate continuum.[5] This point of view may have been articulated most forcefully by a university administrator: "The ideal pattern for professional study is that to which the law school holds. It takes persons with the B.A. degree and *then* becomes concerned with them. It plays no educational role—nor should it—at the undergraduate level."

[5] Werner W. Boehm, *Objectives for the Social Work Curriculum of the Future* (New York: Council on Social Work Education, 1959), vol. 1, chap. 10.

*Chapter 6*


# SUMMARY AND CONCLUSIONS


THIS SERIES OF STUDIES OF THE AMOUNT OF LIBERAL OR NONPROFES-
sional education included in the preparation of future practitioners of
various professional callings was designed primarily to reveal facts with
regard to curricular practices and their justification by the opinions of
those responsible for the controlling policies. Earlier studies consistently
showed wide differences in practice between any two groups of professional schools, as, for example, engineering and journalism, with respect
to the percentage of the undergraduate curriculum devoted to subjects
not directly related to professional activities. Those studies also showed
wide variations from school to school within a given professional field
such as nursing or business administration. Some faculties required that
students concentrate heavily in specialized courses related to practice
while others offered students a strong core of theoretical subjects of broad
professional usefulness and let them pursue other courses in the liberal
arts and sciences according to their interests and abilities. Even within
the same school transcript analysis revealed considerable variations from
student to student in the subject-matter content of their undergraduate
professional preparation.

These divergences between the percentages of the general liberal
courses and the technical professional instruction were markedly narrower in this study of social work education because of the requirement
that the candidate for the degree in social work have completed an undergraduate degree. The differences among institutions with respect to the
emphasis on a liberal arts orientation were also less wide than in other
professional school groups. Although the specific subjects pursued varied
widely in the undergraduate programs of future students of social work the

amount of such preparatory education was much more uniform than in other professions—except those which generally require an undergraduate degree, such as medicine and law. Hence the present study of necessity had to be concerned with the general characteristics of this preparatory education rather than with the wide-ranging proportions of special and general education which characterize preparation for many of the other professions.

The findings in this study cover the attitudes of faculty members and practitioners toward preparatory education in the liberal arts fields. The results also reveal the kinds of courses future students of social work actually pursued in anticipation of the requirements of the graduate schools of social work. Certain other facets of the problem of the balance of liberal and professional studies in the over-all education of the social worker were also treated, such as the history of opinion in the profession on this matter and the views of the central administrative officers toward preparatory education for the practice of a profession.

Insofar as the history of the main issue in the present study is concerned, it can be said that from the earliest days of systematic university education for the practice of social work the vast majority of the leading spokesmen for the profession have favored a sound grounding in the liberal arts subjects. There have in the past been strong advocates of an undergraduate professional course of study and a few still hold to the view that the needs of society, the interests of the student, and the expense in time and money involved in a strictly graduate preparation demand an earlier beginning of professional social work courses. The findings of this study, however, show that this is not the prevailing view.

The statistical analysis of the attitudes of faculty members and administrative officers shows conclusively that there is a large preponderance of opinion favoring a full undergraduate education in the liberal arts and sciences as the optimal preparation for the study of social work at the graduate level. These opinions were generally confirmed in interviews with faculty members in nine graduate schools of social work and with their administrative officers. The facts in Chapter 4 also show little difference between these attitudes and those of directors of undergraduate programs of social welfare, for the latter also favor a liberal arts background for the study of social work. Students in graduate school shared this view as well, but some raised questions about the long period of formal education involved and the value of some types of earlier instruction. There were, however, even among faculty members some who do not wholly agree with the common view. As the data in Chapter 4 show, only 52 per cent of the faculty members believed that a liberal arts degree should be required for admission to a professional school of social work. Moreover, some members of the profession in practice, though valuing liberal studies, were seriously concerned with the inadequate supply of personnel at various levels of practice and the possible restrictive effect of the long period of preparatory education on the available corps of practitioners.

Before attempting to comment on these findings, the relationships established between the kind and the amount of undergraduate education the student pursued and his success in graduate school ought to be summarized. It was found that the amount of instruction the student pursued in any particular field, such as the natural sciences, humanities, or social sciences, had no close statistical relationship to grades received in graduate schools of social work. On the average, students who majored in physics or philosophy maintained just as good records in graduate courses as those who majored in psychology or sociology. There was, however, some positive relationship between high grades in the under-graduate years and in graduate courses. It might be said, therefore, that the profession's general view that a broad liberal education is the best preparation for a graduate professional course in social work is justified by these transcript analyses. It might also be inferred that a prospective social worker could properly be advised to take such courses as his interests dictated, or the undergraduate college required, and to make the highest possible grades in the courses taken, leaving the professional element in his education to later years.

One position of some members of the profession seems called into question by the transcript study. Some schools and individuals advocate a strong concentration in the social sciences. Yet the facts seem to indicate that this type of specialized preparation gives the graduate student in social work no real advantage over his classmates who had only a minimum of prior instruction in the social sciences. This subject is of such obvious importance, and so inconsistent with common sense, that it deserves more detailed analysis and a more determined effort to isolate the factors involved. The fact that the few students who majored in social welfare in the undergraduate period did very well in graduate school, since it conflicts with the common view, also deserves broader study than the number of cases provided in this inquiry made possible. In fact, since many undergraduate social welfare majors are being established in liberal arts colleges the graduates of these programs ought to be studied as they move through their graduate professional programs to determine how they fare relative to the majors in the social sciences, such as sociology and psychology, and to the majors in the non-social science fields. Research projects ought to be inaugurated now in order to make the results of such inquiries available to the profession as soon as enough cases have been analyzed to make valid generalizations possible.

One other major finding in the analysis of attitudes is significant. Of all the various professional groups studied by the Institute of Higher Education the social workers expressed the highest percentage of approval of liberal arts instruction as a basis for professional practice. The unanimity of the profession in this regard is remarkable and seems to assure that social workers of the future are unlikely to come to their professional tasks with a narrow, parochial, how-to-do-it preparation. The social workers, however, tend in one respect to be like members of other professions. Although they strongly endorse a liberal arts degree as preparation for professional courses of study they, like those in other groups, favor courses related to their later professional activities. In order of preference for various types of undergraduate instruction the social work teachers, administrators, and practitioners favor sociology, psychology, history, economics, and political science—all social sciences. Chemistry, physics, and the arts, which have little direct professional application, are favored by only a relatively small percentage of those who responded. The support of liberal arts instruction, even though justified by a strongly declared need for a broad undergraduate education, goes largely to the social sciences which, regardless of their contribution to the purposes of a liberal education, have an obvious utilitarian value in social work. To a degree, therefore, these preferences for specific subject matter deny the general endorsement of a broad, liberal education.

This study may be said to have found that the profession at large continues its dedication to preparatory liberal education. The facts reaffirm its position that the study of professional social work should be reserved for the graduate years. The present practices seem to be confirmed by the fact that the most diverse types of liberal arts curricula prepare equally well for success in the graduate school.

What this study does not do, and what very much needs to be done, is determine the validity of current opinions and practices in terms of the needs of society. Carefully designed and executed research is urgently required to determine whether the weight of current professional opinion is valid. To test the hypothesis that a broad liberal education rather than a more specialized partially professional preparation provides a sounder basis for instruction of the professional school of social work would require a scientifically controlled experiment in which groups of students with and without that preparation competed in identical graduate programs. Then it could be discovered whether a student with two years of liberal arts courses and two years of specialized professional instruction, the kind, for example, commonly given in a school of engineering or business administration, would be as successful in his graduate courses of study in social work as one who pursued no professional courses as an undergraduate; or whether a student with an undergraduate major in social welfare would maintain a record superior to a major in history or physics. The fact that the profession generally looks with disfavor on an early intermixture of liberal and professional courses and thus discourages the kind of experimentation needed to provide valid information on this point makes it very difficult to arrive at conclusions other than those based on opinion. The fact that some medical schools, Johns Hopkins University, for example, have returned at least experimentally to a program which intermixes liberal arts and medical science subjects, rather than making the former exclusively preparatory for the latter suggests that even the profession with the longest history of requiring a bachelor's degree for admission to professional school has had second thoughts on the validity and efficacy of such a requirement.

Lastly, the question of greatest social importance was not touched at all in this inquiry, nor in most others concerned with the validity of undergraduate requirements in preparation for a social work career. That question is, "Does a four-year preparatory course in a liberal arts college, prior to graduate professional study, produce a more competent social worker, or have persons with less than this background performed their professional tasks satisfactorily?" Since they have entered the profession without the standard recommended undergraduate preparation this raises a question about established policy because they apparently have discharged their responsibilities satisfactorily and continue to do so. This is really the question to which practitioners within as well as lay persons outside the profession need a valid answer because they are properly concerned about the shortages of all types of social work personnel, shortages which can hardly be defended on grounds of educational policy when the validity of the answer rests on mere opinion or uncontrolled empirical observation.

To deal with some of these matters, at least on a temporary basis, in January 1962 the Council on Social Work Education published a guide to suggested content, learning experiences, and organization of undergraduate social welfare courses. This was an explicit recognition of the growing importance of undergraduate education in social welfare and provided useful guidelines for the development of courses. It stated that "curriculum content at the undergraduate level would be expected: (1) to contribute knowledge of men and insight into human growth and behavior; (2) to develop knowledge of society and social interaction; (3) to foster an appreciation of the philosophical values which underlie social welfare activities; (4) to develop abilities in methods of problem solving and in the arts of communication; and (5) to provide an understanding of social welfare as one of the professions concerned with human welfare."[1]

There are persons within the profession, a minority to be sure, but a thoughtful and sincere group of competent men and women, who believe that an earlier beginning should be made in the formal education of social workers than is now considered desirable by most of those whose opinions were sought in this study. Their views suggest that objective inquiries such as those being conducted by the National Association of Social Workers and by the United States Department of Health, Education and Welfare ought to be pressed forward with all possible vigor and speed. These inquiries should determine the need for personnel of various types, some of which may be graded at different levels of professional skill. The varieties of formal education required to fill these positions satisfactorily should be determined. These studies should be paralleled with educational research more penetrating and more controlled than has been possible in this study to determine—with facts and figures rather than with opinion—the relationships between various amounts and kinds of undergraduate education and (1) success in graduate schools of social work, and (2) success in the practice of the profession. If this study has underlined the urgent social need for reliable information on this complicated problem it will have served its purpose.

[1] *Social Welfare Content in Undergraduate Education* (New York: Council on Social Work Education, 1962), pp. 3–4.

# *Appendix A*

# SELECTED READINGS

BOOKS AND MONOGRAPHS

AMERICAN ASSOCIATION OF SCHOOLS OF SOCIAL WORK. *Education for the Public Social Services.* Report of the Study Committee of the American Association of Schools of Social Work. Chapel Hill: University of North Carolina Press, 1942. 342 pp.

Stresses the importance of a broad liberal arts foundation for undergraduate students who go on to professional study. It is necessary to study "the scope of the social sciences as a whole, including economics, history, political science, psychology and sociology, rather than a narrow specialization in one field."

AMERICAN ASSOCIATION OF SOCIAL WORK. *Social Work as a Profession.* Revised edition. New York: The Association, 1949. 31 pp.

The best foundation for social work is completion of an undergraduate course of study in liberal arts with a major in the social sciences. Some courses relating to the field of social work may also be given at the undergraduate level, but they should be general and nontechnical.

BISNO, HERBERT A. *The Place of the Undergraduate Curriculum in Social Work Education.* Volume 2 of *The Social Work Curriculum Study.* New York: Council on Social Work Education, 1959. 273 pp.

Discusses the function, content, and organization of undergraduate education in the training of social workers. Believes that an undergraduate social work program can fit within the framework of a liberal arts college, provided that the teaching is "conceptual-analytical" rather than "descriptive-informational."

91

BOEHM, WERNER W. *Objectives for the Social Work Curriculum of the Future.* Volume 1 of *The Social Work Curriculum Study.* New York: Council on Social Work Education, 1959. 416 pp.

Describes the master plan for the study. Draws conclusions from the findings of the project reports, and considers the ways in which their findings overlap or impinge on each other. Discusses the scientific and philosophical bases of the social work curriculum, and charts the distribution of the essential and the desirable in the undergraduate-graduate continuum.

BOEHM, WERNER W., *et al., The Social Work Curriculum Study.* Fourteen volumes. New York: Council on Social Work Education, 1959.

In 1955 the Council on Social Work Education launched an exhaustive examination to see how well the present social work curriculum was meeting the needs of the field in the light of current social work practice. The Study was initiated to: (1) clarify educational objectives of the social work curriculum, (2) illuminate current and future needs of social work education, and (3) help schools of social work and undergraduate departments in the resolution of major current issues in social work education.

BROWN, ESTHER L. *Social Work as a Profession.* 4th edition. New York: Russell Sage Foundation, 1942. 232 pp.

If social work is to be more than a narrow technique, it must have its foundation in the social sciences. A rich undergraduate experience in the social studies is needed.

COUNCIL ON SOCIAL WORK EDUCATION. *Social Welfare Content in Undergraduate Education.* New York: The Council, 1962. 16 pp.

Presents the suggestions of the Council on Social Work Education for the content, learning experiences, and organization of undergraduate social welfare sequences. Emphasis is placed on the desirability of liberal arts education which includes a range of social and behavioral sciences and a sequence of social welfare courses which integrate concepts of the social and behavioral sciences.

COYLE, GRACE L. *Social Science in the Professional Education of Social Workers.* New York: Council on Social Work Education, 1958. 69 pp.

Formulates the contribution which the social sciences can make to social work education. Concludes that the social sciences must provide the basic elements in professional education for social work.

HOLLIS, ERNEST V., AND ALICE L. TAYLOR. *Social Work Education in the United States.* New York: Columbia University Press, 1951. 422 pp.

Contends that "education for professional responsibility is a continuous process which begins in the undergraduate college, is followed by study in a graduate professional school, and is continued after graduation through organized professional association with colleagues." Schools have a responsibility for identifying major concepts of social welfare that belong in our common cultural heritage and are common to all professions, and for a concentration in the arts and sciences basic to graduate professional education. Preparation for social work needs to be liberal, broad, and lacking in overconcentration in any one area.

MADISON, BERNICE. *Undergraduate Education for Social Welfare.* San Francisco: The Frederic Burk Foundation, 1960. 145 pp.

Demonstrates that the process of creating an undergraduate social work curriculum—including content, learning experiences, and organization—can be carried out successfully only within a liberal arts framework.

MCGRATH, EARL J., AND CHARLES H. RUSSELL. *Are Liberal Arts Colleges Becoming Professional Schools?* New York: Bureau of Publications, Teachers College, Columbia University, 1958. 26 pp.

A study of the increasing tendency of liberal arts colleges to add instruction in professional fields, including social work.

TOWLE, CHARLOTTE. *The Learner in Education for the Professions: As Seen in Education for Social Work.* Chicago: University of Chicago Press, 1954. 432 pp.

Professional education is concerned with the development of social sensibility. As preparation liberal arts are a means to enlarge capacity for imaginative consideration, to foster sensitive feeling for people, to give stretch and range to the mind for perception in human relationships and perspective on social change.

TUFTS, JAMES H. *Education and Training for Social Work.* New York: Russell Sage Foundation, 1923. 240 pp.

Schools with graduate programs consider the following to be desirable foundation courses at the undergraduate level: biology and physiology, psychology, history, economics, political science, sociology, and philosophy.

WALKER, SYDNOR H. *Social Work and the Training of Social Workers.* Chapel Hill: University of North Carolina Press, 1928. 238 pp.

Students should have completed undergraduate work before beginning professional training. Social work involves assimilation of a body of knowledge too large and too complex to be part of an undergraduate liberal arts program.

PERIODICALS AND ARTICLES

BOEHM, WERNER W. "Social Work and Social Science," *Mississippi Quarterly,* 9 : 43–55, January 1956.

An undergraduate curriculum should provide the student with a liberal education which whets his appetite for more knowledge, helps him to see life as a problem-solving continuum and himself as a participant in the problem-solving process.

BRANCH, MARY S. "Consultation on Preprofessional Social Work Education," *Compass,* 27 : 12–15, January 1946.

Emphasizes, at the undergraduate level, the essential importance of "a well-rounded liberal arts education with the social sciences in proper relation to the humanities and natural sciences."

BROWNING, GRACE. "The Effect of Modern Developments in Public Welfare on Professional Education and Staff Development," *Social Service Review,* 24 : 51–58, March 1950.

Social workers should receive as much of their education as possible in the liberal arts colleges, and should come to the professional school well prepared in the natural sciences, the social sciences, and the humanities.

CASSIDY, HARRY M. "The Social Science Foundations of Education for Social Work," *Social Forces,* 26 : 303–310, March 1948.

Should aim to give the undergraduate "a decent general education and a reasonable preparation in social science, including some introduction to human behavior and to the social services."

DE SCHWEINITZ, KARL. "Education for Social Security," *Educational Record,* 25 : 142–153, April 1944.

Emphasizes the necessity for "a broad grounding in the social sciences as a culmination of an experience in the liberal arts." The basic need is cultural and not vocational.

FINK, ARTHUR E. "Some Problems of Social Work Education from the Point of View of the State University," *Social Forces,* 20 : 54–64, October 1941.

Social workers need to have the broadest kind of undergraduate grounding prior to receiving professional preparation at the graduate level.

HAMILTON, GORDON. "Some Implications of Social Work Education in the U.S.," *Social Casework,* 33 : 55–60, February 1952.

"The bulk of undergraduate preparation for social work should lie in the humanities and the sciences, with a minimal schedule in technical subject matter. What form of social welfare is not better done by a student with a broad base of knowledge than by one with premature rote knowledge of welfare procedures?"

HATHWAY, MARION. "The Relation Between General Education and Education for Social Work," in *The Thirty-Eighth Yearbook of the National Society for the Study of Education, Part II.* Edited by Guy M. Whipple. Bloomington, Illinois: Public School Publishing Company, 1939, pp. 249–255.

A general education, broad in scope and high in standard, is a minimal guarantee of resources conducive to the development of the professional social worker.

HATHWAY, MARION. "Twenty-five Years of Professional Education for Social Work—and a Look Ahead," *Compass,* 27 : 13–18, June 1946.

"The college graduate who has mastered social science subject matter within a liberal arts education is really the answer to the agency needs which cannot be supplied as yet from the professional schools."

KEATING, VAL M. "Undergraduate Preparation for Social Welfare in the United States," discussion of Sophie T. Cambria's paper in *Education for Social Work,* Proceedings of the Second Annual Program Meeting of the Council on Social Work Education, 1954, pp. 58–62.

In the basic preparation of a public assistance worker there is no substitute for a liberal education. Undergraduate preparation needs to be broad and maturing, as foundation either for graduate social work education or for immediate employment.

KENDALL, KATHERINE A. "Jane Addams: A Product of Liberal Education," *Social Work,* 7 : 84–88, April 1962.

Points out that professional education provides the necessary bridge to professional practice, and liberal education provides the base.

LOWY, LOUIS. "Social Work and Social Statesmanship," *Social Work,* 5 : 97–104, April 1960.

Points to the social worker's need for knowledge and understanding of history, economics, political science, and sociology if he would speak with authority on the wider social issues.

MCGLOTHLIN, WILLIAM J. "The Aims of Professional Education," in *Education for Social Work,* Proceedings of the Sixth Annual Program Meeting of the Council on Social Work Education, 1958, pp. 20–31.

Compares the aims of education for ten professions, including social work. The university is not an appropriate place for the professional school whose objective is to transmit merely technical skills. Professional education needs the stimulus of a research environment, the breadth of contact with various fields, and the support of the liberal arts and sciences.

MCGRATH, EARL J. "Cooperation of Education and Social Work," in *Proceedings of the Seventy-sixth Annual Meeting of the National Conference of Social Work,* 1949, pp. 90–101.

Stresses that professional social work education should be at the graduate level, and based on the intellectual maturity and breadth of learning provided by a balanced liberal arts undergraduate education.

MOSSMAN, MEREB E. "Preprofessional Education for Social Work," *Virginia Public Welfare,* 25 : 4–5, September 1947.

"Undergraduate study which represents the first stage of preparation for professional education in social work should consist of a sound foundation in general education with a concentration in the social sciences and closely related subjects."

ROMANYSHYN, JOHN M. "The Basic Social Welfare Course on the Undergraduate Level: Some Principles and Some Problems," in *Education for Social Work,* Proceedings of the Ninth Annual Program Meeting of the Council on Social Work Education, 1961, pp. 109–122.

Discusses the development of a course on social welfare as a social institution, requiring students to draw on relevant concepts from the social sciences. The course is conceived as having a central place in the liberal arts curriculum.

TANNAR, VIRGINIA. "Training Program in Public Assistance and the Schools of Social Work," *Public Welfare,* 15 : 142–146, 149, October 1957.

The graduate student needs to be broadly based in knowledge from the sciences which form the foundation for social work practice, "that is, the social sciences and the behavioral sciences which give understanding of the social problems in all aspects."

TOWLE, CHARLOTTE. "Issues and Problems in Curriculum Development," *Social Work Journal,* 30 : 67–75, April 1949.

Discusses the importance of continuity, sequence and integration in the educational process beginning in the undergraduate years; the first stage of social work education should be comprised of liberal arts with a concentration in the social sciences.

WETZEL, HAROLD E. "Educational Priorities as Seen by the Undergraduate Department," in *Education for Social Work,* Proceedings of the First Annual Program Meeting of the Council on Social Work Education, 1953, pp. 58–61.

The role of undergraduate social work education must include providing a liberal arts foundation not only for on-the-job training, but for graduate professional education as well.

WISNER, ELIZABETH. "Edith Abbott's Contribution to Social Work Education," *Social Service Review,* 32 : 1–10, March 1958.

A pioneer in the development of graduate social work education, Edith Abbott's addresses and writings emphasize the underlying significance of a broad liberal education to professional preparation for the social services.

*Appendix B*

# INVENTORY OF VIEWS REGARDING LIBERAL AND SPECIALIZED EDUCATION

The Institute of Higher Education
525 West 120th St.
New York, N. Y. 10027
Earl J. McGrath, *Director*

This survey is one phase of a broad investigation of the role of the liberal arts in specialized, professional, or technical curricula. Your response will be helpful to us in assessing the problems and points of view involved in these two related yet distinctive components of higher education.

Please give us the following information about yourself.

Name _____ Birth date _____

Collegiate education: Please list each institution attended, degree earned, and field of major.

| | Institution | Major | Degree | Year |
|---|---|---|---|---|
| 1. | | | | |
| 2. | | | | |
| 3. | | | | |
| 4. | | | | |

What subjects are you teaching in the present term or semester? _____

## PART I

ALMOST every college curriculum can be divided into specialized, technical, or professional courses and those courses classified broadly as liberal or general education. The latter includes courses in the arts, literature, language, social science and natural sciences. By responding to the following statements you are asked to make judgments about the appropriate relation between these two parts of the curriculum both in general and for the special field with which you are involved. To facilitate treatment of responses from a number of people, a separate answer sheet is to be used. Please mark your reaction to each statement by blackening the appropriate space with the special pencil provided.

FOR each statement 1 to 26 blacken
    answer space *1* if you tend to agree.
    answer space *2* if you tend to disagree.
    answer space *3* if you are concerned but undecided about the matter.
    answer space *4* if the issue is one to which you are completely indifferent.

1. All college students, regardless of major or school attended, should be required to take some courses in the liberal arts and sciences which contribute to a liberal or general education.

2. Liberal arts courses to be taken by professional or technical students should be specifically adapted to the needs of such students, such as English for Engineers, or Economics for Business Administration students.

3. More liberal arts courses should be introduced into most technical and professional curricula even if this would somewhat lengthen the time required to earn a degree.

4. In adjusting the balance between liberal and professional requirements, the number of liberal arts courses rather than the number of specialized courses should be reduced.

5. Liberal arts courses develop broad intellectual interests and humanitarian attitudes to a greater extent than do technical and professional courses.

6. Students with broad liberal arts undergraduate training suffer in competition in professional school with students who specialized as undergraduates in a related field.

7. Graduates of specialized curricula in which little attention is given to the liberal arts are often lacking in imagination, in broad perspective, and in ability to see problems outside their own field.

8. There is virtually no difference between the purpose of liberal arts and specialized courses.

9. Persons who have received a broad liberal arts education as well as a technical one have an advantage with respect to future vocational advancement.

10. *Every* professional curriculum should include some courses in the liberal arts and sciences.

11. Even if liberal arts courses are well taught, the values claimed for them are unattainable.

12. All professional or technical students should have a few *free* electives, and each individual may then decide for himself whether he takes any courses in the liberal arts.

13. Instruction in all courses required in a specialized program, whether the courses are liberal arts or specialized, should be given by professors holding appointment in the technical or professional school.

14. Bright technical and professional students will usually pick up during and after college sufficient liberal

arts experience through outside reading, attending lectures, and the like.

15. The benefits claimed for liberal arts courses could be achieved as well or better by well-taught specialized or professional courses planned with some attention to general education objectives.

16. The best education for a technical or professional field is intensive specialization through good courses in that field or directly related to it.

17. Any attempt to combine liberal arts courses with a specialized program destroys most of the value of both.

18. Liberal arts courses are just as specialized as technical and professional courses.

19. Even with the best possible secondary school program, some provision should be made for continuing general education in every post-high school educational program.

20. The attitude of liberal arts professors toward students in technical and specialized curricula is such that it is unfair to these students to place them in liberal arts courses outside of their own school.

21. A liberal arts degree should be a prerequisite for professional curricula.

22. Since many college-age youth are so strongly vocationally motivated, general and liberal education should be postponed and offered through adult education programs.

23. Students majoring in *your* specialty are now commonly required to take an excessive amount of liberal arts work at the expense of needed specialized courses.

24. Students majoring in *your* specialty should be required to take more liberal arts courses than now commonly required, even if that means restricting the specialized part of the curriculum.

25. Students majoring in *your* specialty who take heavier than average course loads in the liberal arts have poorer employment prospects than do those emphasizing specialized training.

26. Students majoring in *your* specialty should be encouraged to meet their liberal arts requirements by taking courses having immediate applications to their vocational field.

## PART II

THE following questions are also to be answered by blackening the appropriate spaces on the attached answer sheet. However, the form of questions differs from the previous group. Select the answer which accords *most nearly* with your own point of view. *Notice that the next question is number 31. Spaces 27, 28, 29, and 30 are to be left blank.*

31. The proportion of a four-year undergraduate technical, pre-professional, or professional curriculum devoted to liberal arts courses should be
   1. 0 to 10%.
   2. 11% to 25%.
   3. 26% to 35%.
   4. 36% to 50%.
   5. over 50%.

32. Which *one* of the following patterns of offering required liberal arts courses do you most favor for professional or technical undergraduate curricula?
   1. All such courses taken during the first two years.
   2. Such courses spread evenly throughout the four-year undergraduate curriculum.
   3. Heavy liberal arts requirement the first year with decreasing amounts each succeeding year.
   4. Heavy concentration of liberal arts in the senior year.
   5. Such courses taken at the convenience of the students.

33. Which *one* of the following ways of providing for the liberal arts education of technical or professional students do you most favor?

1. A limited core of required courses contained within the four-year undergraduate curriculum.
2. Extending the professional curriculum by a summer or an additional year to provide time for liberal arts courses.
3. Offering extracurricular seminars, lectures, concerts and reading groups.
4. Relying on students acquiring a liberal arts education on their own either before or after graduation.
5. Making the first two years of college heavily liberal arts and building thereon appropriate specialized curricula to whatever period of time is appropriate.

QUESTIONS 34 to 51 are names of departments or areas usually listed among the liberal arts and sciences. Indicate your judgment concerning the desirability of *some* work from each area for *students in your own specialty* by selecting one of the five elements of the key and marking your answer sheet appropriately.

KEY: 1. Should be required of all students.
2. Should be optional but encouraged for all students.
3. Should be completely optional for all students.
4. Students should be discouraged from taking work in this area.
5. Students should not be allowed to take work in this area except as an extra course beyond regular requirements.

34. English Composition
35. History
36. Philosophy
37. Biology
38. Physics
39. Chemistry
40. Mathematics
41. Religion
42. Art

43. Literature
44. Psychology
45. Sociology
46. Economics
47. Political Science
48. Music
49. Speech
50. Foreign Language
51. Physiology

FOR these same areas indicate the prevailing pattern for *students in your specialty at the institution with which you are presently affiliated.*

KEY: 1. Some work required of all students.
2. Optional but encouraged for all students.
3. Completely optional.
4. Not recommended for students in my specialty.
5. Credit toward graduation not given for this course.

52. English Composition
53. History
54. Philosophy
55. Biology
56. Physics
57. Chemistry

58. Mathematics
59. Religion
60. Art
61. Literature
62. Psychology
63. Sociology

64. Economics
65. Political Science
66. Music

67. Speech
68. Foreign Language
69. Physiology

WE do not always know what other persons actually believe, but we often have hunches about their beliefs to the point where they influence our conception of possible developments. Questions 70 to 77 are names of positions likely to be found in your present institution. Select from the key the attitude you believe the persons now in these positions hold toward liberal arts courses.

KEY: 1. Believes more liberal arts courses should be required than is currently true, even at the expense of technical parts of the curriculum.
2. Believes enrollment in liberal arts courses should be encouraged but never at the expense of technical parts of the curriculum.
3. Believes liberal arts courses of little value for students in technical or professional fields.

70. President of the instiution.
71. Dean of your specialized school or college.
72. Typical department head in your specialized school or college.
73. Typical faculty member in your specialized school or college.
74. Dean of the school or college of liberal arts and sciences.

75. Typical department head in the college or school of liberal arts and sciences.
76. Typical faculty member in the college or school of liberal arts and sciences.
77. Typical member of the student personnel staff.

QUESTIONS 78 to 85 are the names of these same positions. Indicate the method you believe each of the present occupants of the position would favor in providing technical or professional students with liberal arts education.

KEY: 1. No provision for liberal arts.
2. A prescribed set of courses having direct relevance for the specialized field.
3. Free election from any of the regularly available liberal arts courses.
4. A limited election requiring work in each of the areas of the liberal arts.

78. President of the institution.
79. Dean of your specialized school or college.
80. Typical department head in your specialized school or college.
81. Typical faculty member in your specialized school or college.
82. Dean of the school or college of liberal arts and sciences.

83. Typical department head in the school or college of liberal arts and sciences.
84. Typical faculty member in the school or college of liberal arts and sciences.
85. Typical member of the student personnel staff.
86. Which of the following most clearly

approximates your belief as to the values of liberal arts courses?

1. More should be required even at the expense of some technical courses.

2. Liberal arts courses should be encouraged but rarely at the expense of technical parts of the curriculum.

3. Liberal arts courses are of little real value to students in technical and professional curricula.

87. Which of the following patterns for providing liberal arts education do you favor?

1. No provision for liberal arts other than that inherent in well-taught specialized courses.

2. A prescribed set of courses each having direct relevance for a specialized field.

3. A few broad courses required of all students and designed to acquaint them with the major areas of the liberal arts and sciences.

4. Student free election of courses from within each of three or four areas in the liberal arts and sciences.

5. Student free election from any regularly scheduled liberal arts courses.

The following are statements which could be made about liberal arts and sciences offerings in technical, pre-professional and professional curricula. Select from the key the statements most nearly descriptive of the situation at your present institution. If certain liberal arts or general education courses are already required for students in your field, your response should reflect your view of these courses.

KEY: 1. Typically true at this institution.
2. Cannot make a judgment of this matter.
3. Typically not true at this institution.

88. Liberal arts courses are typically just another kind of specialized education.

89. Liberal arts courses seem genuinely attempting to provide a broad education for students not majoring in those fields.

90. Liberal arts courses for undergraduates are markedly under the domination of the graduate faculties in those fields.

91. Technical and professional students are inclined to feel inferior to other students in their liberal arts courses.